Great
American
Beer

CHRISTOPHER B. O'HARA

Great

American

Beer

50 BRANDS THAT SHAPED THE 20TH CENTURY

photographs by Alethea Wojcik

Clarkson Potter/Publishers
New York

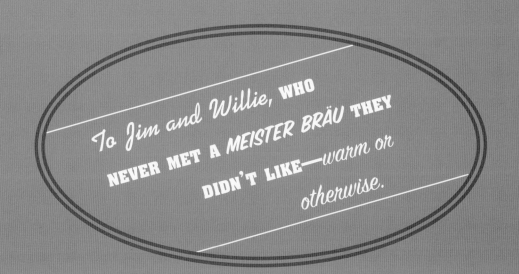

To Jim and Willie, WHO NEVER MET A MEISTER BRÄU THEY DIDN'T LIKE—warm or otherwise.

Acknowledgments

There are quite a few people without whom this book could not have been written. First among them is Maria Gagliano at Clarkson Potter, an extremely adept—and patient—editor who was one of the few people in publishing not to appear dumfounded at the concept of writing a book dedicated to value-priced American beer. Second is my photographer, Alethea Wojcik, a great catalog shooter who brought her considerable skill shooting fashion and accessories to capture rusty beer cans and old coasters. Third (but not in that order) is Erik Amundson. Erik, the owner of one of the best internet sites for feeding beer collectors' weird addiction, was a real partner on this project, and brought his love for all things beer (and his notable collection) to the book on a pro bono basis. I should note that every single item you see pictured in this book is available for sale at Erik's Tavern Trove website, www.taverntrove.com—along with many similar things. So, if you're starting or building a collection of brewery-related items, Erik is a good guy to talk to.

The beer community is a friendly one, and Dale P. Van Wieren is a good representation of what you can expect when meeting a beer scholar. The author of the comprehensive *American Breweries* series of books, Dale's ongoing history of the American brewing industry is unsurpassed, and I reference his work and reproduce, in edited form, his chronology in this book. If this book inspires anyone to take a deeper look into the American beer industry and the effects it has had upon our culture, Dale's books are the place to start. In the same vein, historian Carl H. Miller's work is referenced throughout the book. I would like to thank both Carl and his editor at *All About Beer*, Julie Bradford, for their help getting me access to Carl's incisive commentary on American beer in popular culture. Lastly, I would like to thank the more than 200 friends and random associates from around the country who were involved in the process of creating the list for this book; Jay Sones, my publicist at Potter; and (as always) the unbelievable design team, headed up by the talented Jennifer Beal.

Contents

We are here to drink beer.
We are here to kill war. We are here to laugh
at the odds and live our lives so well that
Death will tremble to take us.

—*Charles Bukowski*

Introduction

My introduction to beer started on a warm summer day in 1982 on a weathered green bench on the Avenue B side of Tompkins Square Park in New York City. The beer was Rolling Rock, a six-pack purchased with astonishing ease at the bodega on 12th Street, and swathed in small brown paper bags—the standard form of concealment for underage drinkers and veterans alike. I twisted off the cap, doffed my beer in my friend Frank's direction, and promptly drained off half of the bottle. We looked at each other and laughed. Of course this was illegal—they would never let anybody our age have this much fun. After finishing the six-pack, we walked back up Avenue B to the basketball courts on 14th Street, reveling in the newfound power of Beer. When we got to the court, I was astonished when I couldn't dunk the ball. The truth was that neither of us was sober enough to even make a layup.

It's funny how that memory takes precedence over so many other "firsts" that happen when you're young. The first kiss. First home run. First concert. Though I didn't know it at the time, that first real drink of beer was my first step on a very long road to adulthood. The irony that my first giant step of individualism consisted of doing something my father did—and learned from his father before him—didn't matter. There is a kind of magic in that first beer. There may be thousands—if not tens of thousands—of beers to remember over a lifetime, but that first beer sticks with you for a long time.

For me, it was a Rolling Rock—at the time, an inexpensive and mysterious selection from the bottom of the bodega's cooler. For you, it may have been Budweiser, or Pabst Blue Ribbon, or maybe even an ice-cold can of Schaefer purloined from your dad's garage fridge. This book is about celebrating the classic beers we encountered in our youth. Not gourmet "sipping" beers like a Belgian *Witbier* or a

FROM PERFECT  BREWING WATER

Kid, we sell enough beer in here to float a battleship.

— Ticket seller at Yankee Stadium bleacher box office, when asked by the author if beer was sold in the bleachers (circa 1999)

Beer

German *doppelbock,* but the classic all-American brews that our fathers and grandfathers drank, like Schaefer, Schlitz, Hamm's, and Rheingold. In so few words, "the beers to have when you're having more than one."

What is it about these stalwart brands that capture our imagination in the way that today's microbrews and other specialty beers do not? In some ways, it is about embracing a time in America when things were much simpler.

Though many of the hallmarks of early twentieth-century America (racism, war, lack of women's rights, etc.) were so inexorably wrong, there was still much to celebrate in the "good old days." It's hard to believe, but there was actually a time when one income could support a family, when American automobiles were top-notch, and when you could get your first—and last—job with a good company and retire comfortably on your pension. Back then, you ate a steak without fear of cholesterol, went on vacation without a Blackberry, and sent your kids off to school without fear of abduction. Back then, you ordered a "cup of Joe" rather than a "tall half-caf mochaccino latte," and you drank *beer.* Not lager, stout, or IPA. Just plain old *beer.*

Great American Beer celebrates the purity and simplicity of classic American brands and the way they continue to resonate today. This book is intended to be the ultimate guide to beer from the era when Milwaukee was the brewing capital of the world and the big names were Schaefer, Schlitz, Rheingold, and Pabst Blue Ribbon. The antithesis of the recent microbrewery revolution in America, this was a time when the major beer powerhouses took control of the brewing industry and, in the grand spirit of American industry, relentlessly quashed the small, independent producers that relied upon local support. This story is about the Americanization of beer, where homogenized brands—grown through a mixture of political clout, industrialization, and marketing might—became the best loved, and most heavily consumed beer brands in the world.

Great American Beer is also about the power of beer in our popular culture and how marketing turned beer—basically a commodity product with very little differentiation at the time—into powerful brands that had their own unique personalities and images. Even if an ounce of Miller Lite has never passed between your lips, I guarantee you know it's the beer that "tastes great" and is "less filling." As a true American beer lover, you also may be aware that Hamm's hails from "the land of sky-blue waters" (wherever they may be) and be able to hum the Rheingold theme ("it's my beer, it's the dry beer…").

Although the marketing battle for beer drinkers' loyalty (and money) has probably been festering since the first brewery opened up in Manhattan (then New Amsterdam) in 1612, the heart of the battle did not begin until the late 1940s, when a curious confluence of events placed beer in the heart of American popular culture. Televisions were enormously expensive at the time—not everybody had them, but they could be found readily in the local tavern where, thanks to the dearth of quality shows, sports programming dominated the airwaves. Add the fact that "the boys" were mostly back from World War II and to be found in large quantities in the taverns, and you have the undeniably perfect setting for a beer commercial: a roomful of men watching baseball in front of a bar.

The 1947 Subway Series between the Brooklyn Dodgers and New York Yankees was mostly seen in standing-room-only taverns. With regional beer sports sponsorships already firmly established, it was only natural for beer companies to saturate the airwaves with characters ranging from Carling's "Black Label Mabel" to the venerable Hamm's Bear, who enjoyed a sixteen-year run as the beer's primary spokesanimal. Through the magnifying prism of television, our love affair with American beer deepened and became more complex as brands took on a fuller life, with an entire range of logos, jingles, characters, and slogans intertwined in our consciousness.

Of course, our love affair with American beer isn't just about advertising. It is also about where we are from. Before the advent of mass marketing and refrigerated trucking, you simply drank the beers supplied from your local breweries. Yet, even though larger breweries have been able to effectively ship and sell beer across the country since the turn of the twentieth century, affection for one's local brew continues to this day. When soliciting suggestions for what great American brands to include in this book, both friends and colleagues fiercely advocated for their local brews—often citing largely experience-based, anecdotal evidence of their superiority, rather than arguing on the merits of craftsmanship or flavor. Naturally, those from upstate New York insisted that Genesee Cream Ale be placed highest in the pantheon of Great American Beer, while friends from Wisconsin were no less forceful in their advocacy of Leinenkugel, insisting that "once the amber goodness of a Leine's penetrates your lips for the first time, you will see clearly that no other beer compares." For some New Yorkers, the fact that Pabst (made in Milwaukee) was sold in Shea Stadium back when the Jets still played there was reason enough to support it as the ultimate American brew.

Unfortunately, the passage of time, the rise of the megabrewers, and the globalization of the economy have made many beloved regional American beer brands things of the past. In their place have risen thousands of smaller specialty microbreweries, brew pubs, and enough imported beer choice and variety to enable someone to have a different beer every day for the next quarter century without fear of repetition. This is a wonderful thing for all beer drinkers, although I suspect that I will always more vividly remember pulling the ring tab on my first PBR than having my first Samuel Adams Winter Wheat Ale. However, the current resurgence of storied brands such as Rheingold and Schaefer—as trendy, upscale beers—reveals that the power of these American icons has not faded over time.

Whether it is a memory of your father sipping beer in his armchair, a television beer commercial, or a fondness for a local sports team's brew of choice, there is something about these classic American beers that resonates within us. I hope this book evokes these memories and helps you appreciate every can you drink a little bit more.

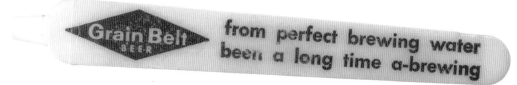

PURITY, BODY, AND FLAVOR IN EVERY GLASS... AMERICA'S LARGEST SELLING ALE...
PURITY
PURITY, BODY, AND FLAVOR IN EVERY GLASS... AMERICA'S LARGEST SELLING ALE...
PURITY
BODY
BALLANTINE'S
PURITY BODY FLAVOR
AMERICA'S LARGEST SELLING ALE
PURITY
BODY
FLAVOR
PURITY, BODY, AND FLAVOR IN
PURITY
BODY
NEW YORK LICENSED OFFICE 295 MADISON AVENUE NEW YORK N.Y.
BALLANTINE'S ALE
© 1942
PURITY BODY FLAVOR
TRADE MARK REG. U.S. PAT. OFF.
XXX
BREWED & BOTTLED BY P. BALLANTINE & SONS NEWARK NEW JERSEY
INTERNAL REVENUE TAX PAID

A Short
of Ameri

History can Beer

THE *Birth* OF *Great American Beers*

Beer has been an integral part of the American landscape since the first Virginia colonists brewed their own corn ale in 1587—and for centuries before, as the Native Americans were known to brew a drink from maize, according to Christopher Columbus. A long-standing legend holds that the Mayflower only touched down on Plymouth Rock because the ship's crew ran out of beer and needed to disembark to obtain the materials to brew more.

Beer was brewed in America continuously since Europeans first set foot on the continent, and the settlers came armed with thousands of years of collective brewing knowledge. The first American beers were ales and stouts—rich, hearty, and robust beers made with top fermenting yeasts at warmer temperatures, then aged for a short time. These were typically heavy British-style brown ales, bitters, and barley-wine, stouts, and wheat beers.

But prior to the mid-1800s, the industry was modest. In 1810, for example, total American beer production stood at a meager 180,000 barrels. It wasn't until the Germans arrived in force throughout the last half of the nineteenth century (over 4 million of them), that the true golden age of American brewing got started and the typical "American-style" beer took hold: smooth and elegant lagers and pilsners.

These new beers were the result of a type of yeast brought from Bavaria: yeast that was active at the bottom of the beer fermenter and worked at much cooler temperatures. When aged in cool caves or cellars, the beer took on a decidedly different character—much cleaner and smoother—than the typical ales of the day. Prior to the mid-1800s, this live

1587
Virginia colonists brew ale using corn.

1607
First shipment of beer arrives in the Virginia colony from England.

1609
American "Help Wanted" advertisements appear in London seeking brewers for the Virginia Colony.

1612
Adrian Block and Hans Christiansen establish the first known brewery in the New World on the southern tip of New Amsterdam (Manhattan).

1620
Pilgrims arrive in Massachusetts aboard the *Mayflower*. Beer is extremely short on board and the seamen force passengers ashore to ensure they will have sufficient beer for their return trip.

Bavarian yeast could not survive the long ocean voyage between the United States and Europe. However, maritime development meant new, fast, multi-sailed clipper ships, which brought enough live yeast—and lively Bavarian brewers with it—to ensure that this style of lager made a swift foothold in the States.

German brewers, supported by a built-in worker and customer base of their fellow expatriates, rapidly took the American beer industry by storm. The combination of their readily drinkable beer, a rapidly expanding European immigrant community with the taste for German lager, and industrious German master brewers transformed the American industry from a comparatively sleepy 750,000 barrels a year in 1850 to an astounding 6,600,000 barrels in 1870—and an estimated 40,000,000 barrels at the turn of the century. That trend was helped along by the fact that the rising immigrant population of America were factory workers prone to drinking before, during, and after their shifts—contributing to a per-capita beer consumption that rose from 6.4 gallons in 1865 to 16 gallons in 1900, and peaked at a (literally) staggering 20.6 gallons in 1910 (according to the U.S. Brewers Association's *Brewers Almanac*).

The German Beer Barons pursued brewing with such a passion that they forever changed the cities their breweries were founded in—and, after a while, all of American culture. With single-minded purpose, they transformed a small cottage brewing industry into the industrial powerhouse it is today: a volume

1637
First authoritatively recorded brewery opens in the Massachusetts Bay Colony under the control of Captain Sedgwick.

1683
William Frampton erects the first brewery in Philadelphia on Front Street between Walnut and Spruce at the Dock Street Creek.

1738
Major William Horton builds the first brewery in the deep south at Jekyll Island, Georgia.

1765
The British Army builds a brewery at Fort Pitt (Pittsburgh, Pennsylvania): the first brewery west of the Allegheny mountains.

business whose product serves the masses. Despite the acuity of their craft and their initial intention to please their fellow German immigrants, the lager beer they produced was aimed at the broadest possible market—everyone. The product that began in the Bavarian countryside won over both the European immigrant population and well-established Americans alike and eventually became what we now call American Beer.

In the cities and towns where they planted roots, the Barons created more than beer. They employed thousands of workers and brought an industriousness that changed the other industries around them. The taverns and saloons they supplied, and often owned, stood as social nexuses in the local communities. The places where they settled (Milwaukee, New York, parts of Pennsylvania) became great beer towns and their ghosts linger on. Being a Beer Baron in the days before Prohibition was like being the President of the United States, Al Capone, and George Steinbrenner all rolled into one. Some of the greatest early stories from New York and Milwaukee give a feeling for the type of men the Barons were, and how they shaped the cities around them.

Milwaukee: Beer City, USA

To the aspiring Beer Baron's eye, Milwaukee was a virtual dreamscape for the intrepid brewer: a welcoming harbor, plenty of ice and cool caves for storage (there was no refrigeration back then), and plenty of thirsty European immigrants. Although Milwaukee was a perfect spot for brewing, it didn't seem to offer any truly unique advantages that couldn't be found elsewhere on the Great Lakes. Yes, it had access to a wealth of wooden barrels, thanks to its proximity to the North Woods. It also had a large immigrant community, but

1765
A brewery is built in the French colonial settlement of Kaskaskia in what is now Illinois. It is the first brewery outside the thirteen colonies.

1775
Revolutionary War measures by Congress include rationing to each soldier one quart of Spruce Beer or Cider per man per day.

1789
George Washington presents his "buy American" policy, indicating he will only drink porter made in America.

1808
Members of the Congregational Church in Moreau, Saratoga County, New York form a temperance society.

so did Chicago. Its water was pristine, but no more so than other nearby industrial centers.

Oddly, Milwaukee's main advantage was what it lacked: enough people to drink all the beer it produced. Milwaukee's brewers quickly ran out of local drinkers, so they learned the crucial art of packaging, shipping, and marketing early. Their first target was Chicago, the city that drank enough Schlitz to "Make Milwaukee Famous."

The other main advantage Milwaukee had was a variety of intrepid, adventurous German brewers who seemed to be armed with risk capital, business acumen, and a magic formula for lager beer. Two of those brewers were Charles and Jacob Best, from Mettenheim, Germany. Starting in 1844, the Best family, owners of a vinegar factory, turned the industrial harbor city of Milwaukee into what would become known as Beer City, USA. In 1844, Jacob Best opened a small brewery on Chestnut Street Hill, which eventually became the Pabst Brewing Company. A few years later, his brother Charles opened a small operation nearby, humbly calling it the Plank Road Brewery. It is now known as the Miller Brewing Company. Sibling rivalry is a wonderful thing.

Other great brewers in the Milwaukee tradition were Captain Frederick Pabst (who married into the Best family), Frederick Miller (who bought the Plank Road Brewery), and Joseph Schlitz. These men, and hundreds of others like them (albeit not as successful), fashioned Milwaukee into a beer paradise. The city was covered with pubs and beer gardens, where free hot lunches, entertainment, and plenty of political votes could be had for the price of a nickel beer. With the great Beer Barons at the hub of the ever-growing German

1826
American Society for the Promotion of Temperance is formed in Boston (also known as the American Temperance Society).

1829
David G. Yuengling opens a brewery in Pottsville, Pennsylvania. It is the oldest operating brewery in the United States, still owned by the Yuengling family.

1833
William Lill & Co. (Heas & Sulzer) start the first commercial brewery in Chicago and produce 600 barrels of ale in their first year.

1836
United States Temperance Union meets in Saratoga, New York, and changes name to American Temperance Union. Principle of total abstinence, or "Teetotalism," is introduced.

community, Milwaukee wallowed in beer and the industry it wrought, creating both larger-than-life characters and beer bellies—humorously known as "Milwaukee Goiter." Truly, Milwaukee was Beer City, USA.

New York: Ehret and the Colonel

The early days of New York brewing can be summed up by two great figures: George "The Crazy Dutchman" Ehret and "Colonel" Jacob Ruppert. In 1857, the twenty-two-year-old George Ehret immigrated to New York City, promptly found employment at a local brewery, and began his rapid climb to the top of American brewing. Fueled by enormous patience, persistence, and frugality, Ehret stashed away his salary (and the knowledge he acquired) from his supervisor position at A. Hupfel Brewery for eight years, until he had enough to start his own operation.

Ehret selected a rural site for his brewery, opposite a dangerous passage in the East River called Hell Gate. Hell Gate Brewery was established with one core principle in mind: to duplicate, as closely as possible, the famous Munich lagers of the day. Finding the local water supply unreliable, Ehret drilled a 700-foot artesian well to draw water for his brewery. The resulting "Franziskaner" beer proved to be an instant hit among New Yorkers. By 1867, the brewery was firmly established and had a wide distribution among New York's numerous bars and taverns. Despite a near crippling setback when his brewery burned to the ground in 1870, Ehret managed to quickly rebuild and nearly doubled his sales every year until the end of the century. Ehret never believed in bottling, so his market was only ever local. However, it is estimated that, by 1900, Ehret was ranked fourth in the nation

1840
Philadelphia brewer John Wagner introduces lager beer.

1847
John Huck and John Schneider start the first lager beer brewery in Chicago.

1849
August Krug forms a brewery in Milwaukee, which evolves into the Schlitz Brewery.

1849
Adam Schuppert Brewery at Stockton and Jackson Streets in San Francisco becomes California's first brewery.

1850
The country's 431 breweries produce 750,000 barrels of beer (31 gallons per barrel). The population is 23 million.

in terms of overall production—even though his sales were limited to New York City.

At roughly the same time of Ehret's ascendancy, another young Bavarian, the ten-year-old Jacob Ruppert, was working for his father's Turtle Bay Brewery and hatching plans for his own operation. When he turned twenty, he asked his father for permission to strike out on his own and, ironically, picked the same desolate spot for his fledgling operation as Ehret did: New York's then-forested Upper East Side, known as Hell Gate.

Starting his operation out of a modest fifty-foot-square brick building, Ruppert sold 5,000 barrels of beer in his first year. A combination of quality beer and relentless salesmanship saw sales of Ruppert's Extra Pale Ale and Knickerbocker Beer rise to 500,000 barrels a year by the mid 1890s, when his son, Young Jake, became general manager of the brewery. A deft politician and salesman, Young Jake was given the honorary title of Colonel by then-Governor Hill. The "Colonel" soon gained a reputation among New York's elite crowd, and his success in New York society mirrored the rapid rise in his beer sales. The Colonel went on to buy the New York Yankees in 1914, built Yankee Stadium (known then, sarcastically, as the "House That Beer Built"), and personally selected the famous Yankee pinstripes for their uniforms. The team (including the later acquisition of one Babe Ruth from Boston) proved to be a sage investment, as Yankee Stadium sold more Ruppert beer than any other location in the country.

In 1935, a triumph greater than the purchase of Babe Ruth sealed Ruppert's destiny as the greatest New York brewer. That was the year George Ehret's heirs sold his brewery to Ruppert.

1852
George Schneider starts a brewery in St. Louis, Missouri. This brewery is the seed of the Anheuser-Busch Brewery.

1852–1854
Prohibition comes to Vermont, Massachusetts (repealed in 1868), Rhode Island (repealed in 1863), Minnesota, Michigan, and Connecticut.

1855
German brewer William Menger starts a lager beer brewery in San Antonio, Texas. This is the first brewery in that city.

1855
Prohibition is adopted in New York, New Hampshire, Delaware, Indiana, Iowa, and the Nebraska Territory.

Across the Country . . .

While Milwaukee dominated the "Golden Age" of brewing, and New York (being New York) was always close to the media spotlight, other parts of the country were also part of the beer revolution. Pennsylvania has been synonymous with beer since its founder, William Penn, built the Pioneer Brew House as his home in Bucks County in 1683. The state also currently holds the distinction of having America's oldest brewery, Yuengling, based in Pottsville and nestled among the Appalachian foothills in Schuylkill County. Philadelphia's Ortlieb is equally distinguished in beer history: the brewery actually stands on the site of where the first lager beer was brewed in America by Bavarian brewmaster John Wagner on Saint John Street, near Poplar, in 1840.

In St. Louis, Adolphus Busch was busying himself with the creation of an international empire built on hops and malt. In Texas, Busch's Lone Star Brewery was fighting for the spotlight with neighboring Pearl Brewing in San Antonio. In Colorado, Adolph Coors was trying to develop the "taste of the Rockies," and further west, Maier and Olympia breweries were wetting the palates of Californians and Washingtonians. German lager beer spread like the flu across America, creating an industry that, with Prohibition, arguably had the biggest impact on domestic American society in the twentieth century. Here is the story of how American beer grew up.

> I would kill everyone in the room for a drop of sweet beer.
> — *Homer Simpson*

1862
Internal Revenue Act taxes beer at the rate of one dollar per barrel to help finance the government during the Civil War.

1862
Thirty-seven New York breweries form an association that will officially become the United States Brewers Association in 1864.

1865
National Temperance Society and Publication House is formed in Saratoga, New York.

1867
John Siebel opens the country's first brewing school, which later becomes the Siebel Institute of Technology.

Pure Artesian Spring Water

HEILEMAN'S

PURE GENUINE

Old Style

Brewed with Water from When the Earth was Pure

1868
Publication of *The American Brewer* magazine, the first beer trade publication, begins in January.

1872
First brewery workers' strike occurs in New York City.

1873
Adolphus Busch begins bottling beer for large scale shipments at the Anheuser Brewery in St. Louis (bottling was not new—it was this venture's magnitude that made it unique).

1875
Louis Pasteur publishes "Studies on Beer," showing how yeast can be controlled.

1880
U. S. Brewers Academy is established.

1886
National Union of the Brewers of the United States is established.

1886
Abraham Cohen establishes the first brewery in Alaska at Juneau.

THE *Rise* OF THE *Great American Beers* OF THE *Twentieth Century*

Death of the Local Brewery

The story of the birth of the great American beers is truly the story of the first microbrewery revolution. The Bavarian master brewers, armed with brewers yeast and secret family recipes, created small-batch beers for limited populations, distributed through a few outlets. With no refrigeration and no easy access to ice, the brewing season was limited, and beer could only travel a short distance before it turned stale. Before the great American beers of the twentieth century could truly emerge, they had to adapt and survive two of the most radical changes in the industry: the emergence of refrigeration and mass bottling, which changed the business environment from regional to national; and Prohibition, a law intended to destroy their business entirely.

The brewers that would eventually survive and create the great American beer brands that still exist today were perhaps better industrialists, politicians, and marketers than craftsmen. Beer was a business—and a serious one at that. With approximately 3,000 breweries in operation in 1867, brewers and industrialists had already developed a large infrastructure of suppliers, distribution outlets, and equipment manufacturers. When the Siebel Institute of Technology, the first accredited brewing school, opened in 1867 and *The American Brewer*, the industry's first trade publication, debuted a year later, the business of beer was truly institutionalized.

1887
Master Brewers' Association is organized.

1888
Brewery employees strike in New York, Chicago, and Milwaukee.

1888
One of the first big brewery mergers takes place. Franz Falk Brewing Company and Jung and Borchert in Milwaukee merge to form Falk, Jung & Borchert Brewing Company.

1889
Eighteen St. Louis breweries merge into the St. Louis Brewing Association.

1889
Six New Orleans brewers combine to form the New Orleans Brewing Company.

1890
British syndicates start price wars. Prices in Chicago decrease from $6.00 per barrel to $3.50 and $4.00 per barrel.

With the second generation of Bavarian brewing masters coming into their own, well-financed and backed by a growing industry support system and knowledge base, brewing became a high-stakes game where quantity and distribution reach trumped craft expertise. By 1873, when a record 4,131 breweries were operating, Busch—the one Beer Baron who was trained as a salesman rather than a brewer—seized the future of beer by bottling and shipping it on a scale not seen before. The game changed forever.

It would only take a few years before Louis Pasteur's *Studies on Beer* showed the industry how to control living yeast organisms and keep beer relatively fresh over long periods of time. Pasteur basically solved the beer problem by killing the living organisms inside beer with heat—simply bottling the beer and immersing the bottles in water hot enough to kill the yeast organisms. Unfortunately, the heating had the effect of "overcooking" the beer, and did not tend to improve flavor. Despite this, brewers now had the ability to package and ship their products across the country, ensuring that the beer tasted the same from origin to destination. Although draft beer, by its very nature, was fresher tasting, it could not compete on a business level. By 1880 the number of brewers had declined to just over 2,800, as the larger brands expanded across the country with packaged beer, slowly pushing mom and pop regional brewers out of business. By 1910, a thousand more regional breweries had succumbed to the trend, and the estimated number of breweries had shrunk to 1,500.

As the marketplace continued its merciless elimination of smaller operations, another disturbing trend was taking hold: Prohibition. Although national Prohibition did not happen until the 1919 Volstead Act took effect, "temperance" movements had been well underfoot for nearly a century. Nickel pints of lager flowing freely through America's vast saloon

1892
Crown cap is invented by William Painter of Crown Cork and Seal Company in Baltimore.

1892
Anti-Saloon League is founded by Reverend Howard Hyde Russell with the goal of suppressing the saloon.

1898
The Royal Brewery is the first to operate in Hawaii.

1898
The Pittsburgh Brewing Company is formed with the consolidation of twenty-one Pittsburgh brewers.

1901
Ten Boston brewers merge into the Massachusetts Breweries Company, Ltd. Sixteen Baltimore brewers consolidate into the Gottlieb-Bauernschmidt-Straus Brewing Company.

infrastructure came with their own consequences: lots of public drunkenness, crime, and prostitution. As early as 1829, the American Temperance Society's 100,000-strong member base was pushing for the abolition of what they saw as a morally bankrupt saloon culture. By 1833, with the German beer invasion just starting to take hold, membership in America's various temperance societies had surpassed one million members. Initiatives on the state and local levels weren't always successful, but Maine's enactment of its 1846 prohibition law was a dark cloud on the horizon for brewers everywhere.

Various temperance experiments waxed and waned in the 1850s, seeing Vermont, Rhode Island, Michigan, Connecticut, New York, New Hampshire, Indiana, Delaware, and Iowa all enact laws with various prohibition measures (many later repealed), but the beer industry got an early taste of what was to come. Luckily for brewers and beer drinkers alike, the newly created Internal Revenue Service's enactment of a dollar per barrel beer tax—primarily for funding Civil War operations—gave state and local governments a convenient excuse to look the other way.

Syndication

Although formal Prohibition was still years away, there was another, more powerful, trend taking hold in the brewing industry that would forever doom the small brewer: syndication. With beer, like any other manufacturing industry, the game is about scale. Larger brewers sought expansion through the acquisition of less cash-rich enterprises. Why spend thousands to build new manufacturing facilities and market new brands, when smaller breweries could be acquired and folded into an already successful business model? Such was the fate of many smaller brewers in the late 1800s.

1905
Independent Brewing Company is formed by fifteen Pittsburgh breweries.

1917
District of Columbia passes a prohibition law.

1919
Eighteenth Amendment to the U.S. Constitution is ratified on January 16, calling for national prohibition to take effect one year from the date of ratification.

1919
House of Representatives presents Bill No. 6810, establishing the apparatus for the enforcement of Prohibition. The bill is vetoed by President Wilson on October 27 but overridden by Congressional vote.

1920s
Near-beers are brewed during Prohibition: Pablo by Pabst, Famo by Schlitz, Vivo by Miller, Lux-O by Stroh, and Bevo by Anheuser-Busch.

With muscular brewing syndicates controlling large areas of distribution and enjoying large economies of scale in manufacturing, the price wars started. Fierce competition between these new regional super brewers kept prices low, which created more syndication. By 1916, almost every brewery region in the United States had consolidated; regional super brewers included Pittsburgh (with twenty-one breweries forming the Pittsburgh Brewing company and fifteen folded into the Independent Brewing Company), Boston (a syndicate of ten brewers), Baltimore (sixteen), and San Francisco (six).

Prohibition

Bill Number 6810, introduced by Representative Andrew Volstead, established the apparatus for enforcing Prohibition. Although it was subsequently vetoed by President Wilson, the veto was overturned, and the Volstead Act authorized the enforcement of the Eighteenth Amendment. Prohibition officially began less than a year later, in 1920, and was the force that would shape American beer for the next century. One of the first major effects of the law was found in local drinking establishments.

In the early days, it seemed as though any brewer with a half-decent product could sell as many cases of beer as he could manufacture. Most brewers pushed their beer through networks of saloons, a marvelous distribution strategy—but one that proved for many brewers to be a fatal weakness. Prohibition, pushed through largely by the advocacy of the Anti-Saloon League, aggressively targeted taverns and beer gardens, which were known for their licentiousness.

1920s
Association Against the Prohibition Amendment is organized by William H. Stayton.

1920
Three hundred million gallons of near-beer are produced.

1923
Montana votes to repeal the state prohibition enforcement law.

1929
The Women's Organization for National Prohibition Reform starts.

1930
The Crusaders, a group protesting the lawlessness and crime brought on by Prohibition, forms.

1930
American Brewers Association is formed.

1933
The Cullen Bill is passed in March, allowing states that did not have state prohibition laws to sell 3.2 percent beer. It also institutes a five-dollar-per-barrel tax on beer.

According to Peter McWilliams, author of *Ain't Nobody's Business If You Do: The Absurdity of Consensual Crimes in a Free Country,*

Saloons were seen as hotbeds of **corruption, contagion**, and **vice**. These male-only (except for "dance-hall girls") establishments were, to the pious, positive hell holes. Drinking, gambling, prostitution, tobacco smoking, tobacco chewing (and its natural by-product, spitting), dancing, card playing, and criminal activity of all kinds were all traced to the saloon. Saloons were irresistible temptations to the otherwise righteous and virtuous men of the community. Invited there for a social drink by the "recruiters of Satan," the young men of the community found themselves hopelessly caught in a spider's web of immorality, lust, and depravity. Alcohol (a.k.a. the devil) was the spider at its very center. The Anti-Saloon League was formed, "an army of the Lord to wipe away the curse of drink."

The small "independently-operated" taverns could be closed on the local level and posed less of a legal burden on enforcement than going after the well-funded brewers themselves. While Prohibition managed to slash incidences of liver cirrhosis by 63 percent, it also had slashed the number of breweries by half by the time it ended in 1933. Only the strong, well-funded breweries that had amassed large fortunes survived.

Breweries with an excess of capital and some imagination survived the long drought. Some produced "near-beers," low-alcohol "cereal" beverages, sodas, chocolate, or malt syrup during the Prohibition years. Near-beer was about as close to real beer as most people

1933
Thirty-one brewers are back in operation by June.

1934
756 brewers are back in operation.

1935
American Can Company and Krueger Brewing Company introduce canned beer.

1935
Schlitz introduces the cone top can, produced by Continental Can Company.

1935
Falstaff Brewing Company of St. Louis leases the Krug Brewing Company of Omaha, Nebraska. This touches off a wave of acquisitions by large brewers.

1940
Beer production is at the level of pre-Prohibition years, with half the number of breweries in operation as in 1910.

IN SUN VALLEY,
SKIING LEADS
...IN MILWAUKEE,
BLATZ LEADS

*...and Blatz Is Milwaukee's
Most Popular Bottle Beer*

HAVE you ever tried a *full-flavored* Pilsener beer? Pale golden of crystal clarity...made with the choicest hops...aged and blended to perfection...it's the result of 90 years' brewing experience. And today it's even better than ever. Order Blatz from your dealer.

BLATZ BREWING COMPANY, MILWAUKEE, WIS.
90 years of brewing experience—established 1851

Even Better Than Before

In Brown
or Clear
Bottles and
in Cans

Blatz
OLD HEIDELBERG BEER

could get, and brands like Pablo (Pabst), Vivo (Miller), and Bevo (Anheuser-Busch) received a mildly enthusiastic response in the marketplace. Using their well-established political clout garnered from years of donations, some of the majors (most notably Pabst and Anheuser-Busch) managed to obtain special federal licenses granting them the ability to produce malt syrup—the base material for home brewing—ostensibly for "medicinal purposes." This highly cynical legislative loophole not only helped fuel alcohol consumption—which was growing, not declining—in the States, but also enabled the major breweries to retain their brewmasters and key brewing personnel, giving them a decided advantage in the post-Prohibition years.

In the meantime, thousands of brewers were closing their doors. In 1930, with winds of change on the horizon, the industry teamed up to create the American Brewers Association to lobby for the brewers that would eventually survive. But with America's taste for near-beer at an all-time low by 1932 (consumption was down 75 percent in volume over the last decade), it would take the repeal of Prohibition to rescue a dying industry.

The Cullen Act of 1933, which allowed states without specific prohibition laws to sell 3.2 percent beer (the beginning of the end of Prohibition, which was eventually abolished with the

1941
All brewers' associations are united under the United States Brewers' Association.

1949–1958
185 breweries close down or sell out.

1951
Anheuser-Busch of St. Louis builds a new brewery in Newark, New Jersey, starting a trend for expansion of breweries.

1954
First 16-ounce can is introduced by Schlitz.

1959
Aluminum can is introduced by Coors of Golden, Colorado.

1960
Aluminum can top is introduced.

1961
230 breweries are operating. Only 140 are independently run.

Twenty-First Amendment) was also a financial bonanza for the government, which realized a highly regressive tax of five dollars per barrel. Despite this onerous fact, the Act was greeted with tremendous enthusiasm by the vast majority of citizens. The "Noble Experiment" of Prohibition had proven to be a complete failure: not only did it not stop people from drinking (it actually increased it to levels not yet surpassed today), but gave birth to widespread government corruption and organized crime as we know it.

Post-Prohibition: Rise of the Great American Beers

Not only did Prohibition knock out under-funded brewers, it also actually helped the major players gain skills they would have otherwise not naturally accumulated, leading to the hyper-consolidation of the business in post-temperance days. For example, although soda beverages were being bottled for years, the beer industry lagged far behind in terms of their ability to bottle and distribute product. Beer was traditionally kegged and shipped to taverns, a less expensive and thus more profitable enterprise. When Prohibition forced brewers to turn to the production of "malt beverages," they began to closely emulate the models of soda producers' bottling and distribution operations. The lessons of this experience weren't lost after Prohibition ended. The statistics tell the story: while 85 percent of pre-Prohibition beer was kegged, nearly 85 percent of near-beer, beer, and soda sold after Prohibition was bottled.

Prohibition also taught brewers the canned goods industry. Suddenly forced to produce what were essentially foodstuffs (syrups and the like), the industry had to adapt to the methods of producing and packaging food products. Blatz adapted quickly and in 1925 was already earning $1.3 million on canned syrup products. By 1935, the American Can

1962
"Tab top" can is introduced by Pittsburgh Brewing Company.

1965
"Ring pull" can is introduced.

1969
Fritz Maytag takes ownership of the Anchor Brewing Company in San Francisco, California. It is not obvious at the time, but a revolution has begun. He brews high quality beer for nonmainstream tastes.

1969
Canned beer outsells bottled beer for the first time.

1971
Philip Morris Company acquires Miller Brewing Company.

1977
The first ale is served in a new brewery in Sonoma, California. The New Albion Brewery will become known as America's first "microbrewery," or "craft brewery."

Company would forever change the beer landscape by introducing the beer can.

With bottling came packaging—another new art to be learned by the brewer. With a long history of well-established and loyal distribution channels, brewers never really had any need to differentiate their products. Beer was typically shipped in identical wooden kegs, and taverns pushed the products they were contractually obliged to carry. One of the caveats to the Twenty-First Amendment, however, made it illegal for brewers to own their own saloon networks. This forced the industry to rely upon a network of distributors, who sold directly to retailers. Now, with sales totally outside of their direct control, a brewery needed to shape its identity to earn retailer loyalty. Thus, packaging in the brewing industry was born.

A key advantage for the large breweries was that their large distribution networks depended on motorized trucking—a relatively new form of shipping, even in 1920. Without a proper supplier for the specific vehicles needed, companies like Anheuser-Busch began to actually manufacture their own trucks—enabling them to customize their shipping operations to exactly meet the needs of their vendors. Needless to say, it was only the largest and most well-capitalized companies who had the wherewithal to accomplish the building of their own delivery fleet.

There were only a few "shipping" beer companies prior to Prohibition (Blatz, Pabst, and Anheuser-Busch), and it is no surprise that these were the companies to be reckoned with after the drought ended. When the industry reawakened, breweries opened up to a radically altered landscape—one in which the major brewers had a serious competitive advantage. Although hundreds of local breweries reopened, they did so in an alien landscape where

1982	1983	1983	1984
For the first time since Prohibition, a brewery opens that not only sells beer on premises, but serves food to boot. In Bert Grant's Yakima Brewing and Malting Company, Inc., the brew pub is born.	In January, fifty-one brewing concerns are operating a total of eighty breweries. This is the low water mark for breweries in the twentieth century.	The top six breweries (Anheuser-Busch, Miller, Heileman, Stroh, Coors, and Pabst) control 92 percent of U. S. beer production.	Microbreweries begin to spread: Riley-Lyon (AR), Boulder (CO), Snake River (ID), Millstream (IA), Columbia River (OR), Kessler (MT), Chesapeake Bay (VA).

the rules of the game had been altered by a dozen years of both repression and innovation; the majority of small brewers ultimately died. In five short years, the number of active breweries declined by 10 percent.

As the U.S. population surged, beer consumption increased; in 1935 it was at levels approaching that of 1910—roughly 60 million barrels. However, with 30 million more people in the U.S. market, per-capita beer consumption was down significantly. For the major brewers of the day it didn't matter; they grew the fastest and controlled the lion's share of the business. In 1938, the leading manufacturers were Anheuser-Busch (2.1 million barrels); Pabst (1.64 million); Schlitz (1.62 million); New York's Ruppert (1.4) and Ballantine (1.1) breweries; Schaefer (1); Hamm's (.750); Pennsylvania's Duquesne Brewing (.625); Falstaff (.622); and Liebman, the maker of Rheingold (.625).

This basic lineup would remain unchanged for a little while—and even prosper through World War II, as the war proved to be a panacea for most manufacturers. The long hangover of the Prohibition and Depression was thrown off and, even in the midst of world war, beer consumption grew at the staggering rate of 50 percent between 1940 and 1945. The war years were truly glory days for big brewing.

After the war, the industry entered a state of consolidation not seen since the late 1880s. Between the end of World War II and 1970, the number of breweries in America shrank from 468 to 154, an amazing tale of consolidation,

1984
Manhattan Brewing Company, in New York City's SoHo district, becomes the first brew pub on the East Coast.

1990
Producing 31,000 barrels of beer, the Sierra Nevada Brewery becomes the first start-up microbrewery to break out of that classification (considered 25,000 barrels or less).

1994
It becomes legal to put the alcohol content of beer on containers.

1995
Approximately 500 breweries are operating in the United States, and they are estimated to increase at a rate of three or four per week.

acquisition, and attrition. In fact, it took only twenty-five years (a short breath in an industry with four centuries under its belt) for the top five brewers to go from having 19 percent market share to owning over 64 percent of the American market (a number that is over 85 percent today). A large amount of that growth and consolidation can be directly attributed to the creation of the beer can by the American Can Company in 1935.

The invention of the beer can was the final blow to small, regional brewers. This marvelous device, coupled with the mass availability of household refrigeration, enabled consumers to enjoy ice-cold and fresh beer straight from their kitchens. This modern convenience caused a sea change in an industry that, until as late as 1935, had relied on draught beer for 70 percent of its sales volume.

1996
Craft beer year-over-year growth begins to slow from 51 percent in 1995 down to 26 percent in 1996.

1998
Craft brewing growth levels out, representing about 3 percent of the total American beer market, where it will stay for the foreseeable future.

2001
Guinness test-markets canned beer that features a self-activating "widget" of nitrous within the can to produce an instant draft beer.

2001
Alaska-based manufacturer Incan comes out with a heat sealed, ziplock foil pouch that can substitute for a beer bottle.

By the end of the war, canned and bottled beer accounted for more than 64 percent of sales. By 1970, canned and bottled beer was more than 85 percent of total beer sales by volume, according to the U.S. Brewing Association.

Americans loved canned beer, and the industry continually strived to meet their needs. In 1935, Schlitz introduced the famous "cone-top" can—the beer can with the characteristics of a bottle. In 1954, Schlitz introduced the sixteen-ounce can, which continues to be an industry staple at convenience stores this very day. Coors, always an industry innovator, brought the aluminum can to market in 1959 and, in 1962, Pittsburgh Brewing marketed the first "tab top" can, making packaged beers easier to open. Only three years later, the "ring pull" can came on the market, and the novelty never really wore off; by 1969, canned beer was outselling bottled beer for the first time in history.

By 1970, the Great American Beers were firmly established in the national consciousness (and refrigerator). With help from television advertising, an ever-expanding national highway and rail system, and—most importantly—sports advertising, brands like Budweiser, Miller, Coors, Pabst Blue Ribbon, Schaefer, Stroh's, Blatz, Schlitz, and Rheingold were household names. So, too, were the regional beers that were lucky enough to be enveloped under the major company's brand portfolios or just good enough to survive on their own: Rolling Rock, Rainier, Leinenkugel, and Ballantine.

2002
Anheuser-Busch's stock rises 7 percent—while the Dow Jones Industrial Average sinks 17 percent.

2003
The total United States market sells a stunning 204,333,000 barrels of beer.

2004
40 percent of Americans admit to considering low-carb diets. Sales of low-carb beers like Michelob Ultra, Rolling Rock's Green Light, and Coors's Aspen Edge explode. The total beer market contracts, however, as the diets prohibit all beer drinking.

The Greatest American Beers

The following list represents only a subjective opinion of what comprises the fifty greatest American beer brands of the twentieth century and is, by its very nature, exclusionary. Why fifty, anyway? Well, fifty is a nice, round, American number, and when people ask for a list of something you are usually looking for the "top ten" or "top one hundred." The size of this particular book and other publishing constraints made this list come out to fifty. There are some very good—indeed, historic and classic—beers not included in this list (my original "short list" topped out at about 120).

I have tried to identify the fifty brands that were either highly recognizable, made an impact on the beer industry, had a strong regional following, or were just plain, tasty American beers (or all of the above). That being said, the criteria for the list are pretty specific: the brand has to be American, in existence prior to 1975, and brewed on a fairly large scale. That means there are no microbrewery beers or specialty "craft" beers included in this list. If you are after that sort of information, then you are looking for a book by Michael Jackson (no, not the Gloved One), the preeminent authority on beer, and the author of the excellent books *Ultimate Beer* and *Great Beer Guide* (and many, many more).

The list of fifty is in two sections: "Pioneers of Beer," focusing on the key mega brands that started mass brewing, and "The Great American Beers," comprised of classic regional brands that, for the most part, are still around today. In almost every case, each brand has a long and storied history and a deep association with the city or town in which it is (or was) brewed, and weathered both the Great Depression and Prohibition to enter the era of modern brewing.

Also included is a bit of the history, to give a feeling for the rich background and accomplishments of some of these brands. I think some of the stories will be surprising to those of us who may ordinarily be inclined to give these brands no more than a cursory glance in the beer cooler as we pick out our six-packs of Stella Artois and Samuel Adams.

America
Timeles

's Most
s Brands

Pioneers of Beer

The Brands That Started It All

BUDWEISER

By: Anheuser-Busch Brewing Company
Where: St. Louis, MO
From: 1860–Present
AKA: Bud
Slogans: "The King of Beers"
　　　　　"This Bud's for You"

This is the famous Budweiser beer. We know of no brand produced by any other brewer which costs so much to brew and age. Our exclusive Beechwood Aging produces a taste, smoothness, and a drinkability you will find in no other beer at any price.

—Budweiser Manifesto

Overview

Apple pie. NASCAR. Mom. Bud. In the American lexicon, there are only a few words as iconographic as "Bud." The number one beer in the world, much of the success of Budweiser can be traced to its masterful marketing.

　　Its early advertising positioned the brand as "more than beer, a tradition." Budweiser was one of America's first brands that truly became more than the sum of its parts. Just as one thinks of "Kleenex" as another word for tissue, one almost automatically visualizes a can of Budweiser when hearing the words "American beer." Perhaps the greatest marketing innovation Bud was responsible for were the words: "For all you do, this Bud's for you." Borrowing from Miller's groundbreaking "If you've got the time, we've got the beer" campaign, Bud's catchy slogan reinforced the idea that you *deserved* a beer—a universal

concept that still resonates with hard working (and drinking) men across the world.

During the 1987 Superbowl, Budweiser gave birth to the modern era of the advertising mascot with Spuds McKenzie, the "official party animal" of Bud Light. In the 1990s, Spuds's huge success was followed by Bud's inexplicably popular "frogs" commercials, featuring three swamp frogs that were able to croak out the syllables "Bud-Weis-Er" as a team and tongue-grab ice-cold bottles of Bud. The frogs were followed by the even less subtle team of Frank and Louie, an odd-couple of talking lizards, who were portrayed as jealous of the frogs' spokesanimal status. Clearly, Bud had become more than a brand of beer; Bud was conceptual—an idea meant to convey humor and good times. Bud's ads cemented that concept and helped keep Bud the number one beer in the world, a position it still enjoys today.

It was also in the 1990s (1996, to be precise) when Budweiser introduced its "born-on" dating system, in which every bottle and can of Bud was laser-printed with the date of its conception. Widely hailed as a brilliant marketing move, the born-on dates assured consumers that Bud was the freshest product on the shelves—making all other choices unknown quantities. Most consumers embraced the revolutionary strategy, not realizing that Lucky Lager introduced the idea nearly sixty years earlier, when it started labeling every can and keg with the date it left the factory.

History

Adolphus Busch, the man who would eventually reign supreme as the "King of Beers" was a salesman in the brewer's supply business.

In the 1850s, it was to Busch's great fortune that one of his customers, Eberhard Anheuser, a soap manufacturer trying his hand at brewing, went deeply into debt to him. Unable to pay Busch's mounting invoices, in 1860 Anheuser offered a percentage of his brewery in exchange for a clean slate. Busch quickly seized upon the opportunity—and Anheuser's daughter, Lily. The two were married shortly thereafter, permanently cementing the Anheuser-Busch family relationship.

Young Busch quickly went about the business of setting the struggling brewery to rights. In 1865, the brewery was producing a scant 8,000 barrels a year of sub-standard beer in a market—newly flooded with German immigrants—that was consuming millions of gallons. At the time, the true King of Beers in St. Louis was William Lemp. Armed with a superior brew and a vast network of taverns and beer gardens in which to vend it, Lemp posed a formidable challenge for the fledgling brewery. But in the end, even Lemp was not immune to Busch's considerable political skills and salesmanship.

As the legendary story has it, Busch's friend Conrad, a local wine merchant, encountered a beer in Bavaria from a small monastery and paid for the recipe. Returning to St. Louis, he turned the recipe over to the Busch brewery in lieu of some unpaid bills. The beer was named after the small town of Budweis, where the recipe was discovered. Thus, Budweiser was born.

The miracle of pasteurization occurred at the same time in the 1870s, allowing bottled beer to travel across the country without spoiling. Now, the stage was set for the greatest traveling salesman of all time to make his beer a national sensation. It wasn't long before Busch had installed Anheuser-Busch's Budweiser beer in every city in the Union, and most of the civilized world. The St. Louis brewery grew to an astonishing 142 acres of land and employed over 7,500 men to brew over 1.5 million barrels of beer a year—90 percent of which were for the foreign market. Budweiser's surging popularity allowed Busch to focus on a few, successful brands, including his Pale Ale, Faust, and Michelob. By this time, the Lemp family and their formidable Falstaff beer was a far second place; and among all American brewers, Anheuser-Busch had no significant rivals.

PABST BLUE RIBBON

By: Pabst Brewing Company
Where: Milwaukee, WI
From: 1844–Present
AKA: PBR
Slogans: "It's Blended . . . It's Splendid"
"What We Drink Around Here"

Overview

The Pabst story began in 1844 and is still a vibrant part of the American beer landscape today. Like many historic American beers, Pabst had its heyday in the 1950s, when it was a respected, solid, pilsner-style beer for the regular guy. Up until the 1970s, Pabst competed nationally with other popular brands, such as Budweiser, Miller, and Coors. Now, Pabst is a cult phenomenon, with millions of loyal adherents who embrace the brand as the American über-beer, the diametric opposite of trendy imports and snobby "craft-brewed" beer. Ironically, its iconic "everyman" status has made Pabst itself trendy, but mostly among the college crowd. Pabst owes much of its recent cult status to Dennis Hopper's homicidal Frank Booth character in the movie *Blue Velvet*, who proclaims his great love for domestic beer by screaming: "Heineken? Fuck that shit! Pabst Blue Ribbon!"

History

The Best brothers' first stab at brewing began in 1844 when Jacob Best returned from his ancestral home in Mettenheim, Germany, and opened a small brewery on Chestnut Street Hill in Milwaukee called Best and Company.

Jacob's brother Charles left the brewery soon after its inception, and went back to making vinegar with his other brothers. The pull of the brewery business proved stronger than his intentions, however; five years later he and his brother Lorenz established the Plank Road Brewery. That brewery is now known as the Miller Brewing Company.

Phillip Best and Captain Fred Pabst

Under the flag of Best and Company, the Best family gradually increased the production—and quality—of their beer, until they were ranked fourth overall in terms of Milwaukee breweries, producing more than 2,500 barrels of beer a year. By that time, Jacob Best was ready to retire. He chose as his successor the son he felt had the best beer making instincts and large-scale plans for its future, Phillip Best. Under Phillip's sole proprietorship, both the business and his health fared poorly, leading many to speculate that Best Brewing was doomed to failure.

Enter Captain Fred Pabst, an acquaintance of Phillip—and eventually his son-in-law, through his marriage to his daughter, Maria, in 1859. A Great Lakes steamship captain who had no intention of leaving his chosen profession, fate forced Captain Pabst into the brewery business when a violent lake storm destroyed his steamship. Accustomed to frequent travel, the captain capitalized upon his newly purchased 50 percent stake in the brewery by traveling across the United States and Europe to secure financing and equipment for the brewery—and to purchase smaller brewers to fold into the ever-widening Phillip Best Brewing Company, which would eventually become Pabst Brewing.

Over the years, Captain Pabst further consolidated his business, operating two breweries at full steam and broadening his empire to include over forty regional sales offices around the country. The year 1878 brought Pabst international success at the Paris World's Fair, where the Pabst brand won several medals. The rest is history.

MILLER

By: Miller Brewing Company
Where: Milwaukee, WI
From: 1855–Present
Slogan: "The Champagne of Beers" (Miller High Life)
Song: "If you've got the time, we've got the beer."

Sometimes a man gets too hungry to clean his hands properly. The powdered sugar on this doughnut puts a semi-protective barrier between your fingerprint and your nutrition. But even if some grease does get on that doughnut, well, that's just flavor to a High Life man.

—Miller High Life Ad (Weiden + Kennedy)

Overview

In 1971, those gathered for Miller's national sales meeting were introduced to a brand new concept: beer ads that focused on the drinkers, rather than the beer. "If you've got the time, we've got the beer" was the slogan (and jingle), which made it clear that, after a hard day of work driving a forklift or humping a jackhammer, you *deserved* that beer, and Miller High Life was your brand. Budweiser followed with "This Bud's for You," and the culture of "know your customer" was born.

Even more impressive than Miller's 1971 campaign was its deft approach in marketing light beer, then an unknown entity. How would Miller market a diet beer to their customer base of "real men" who seemed no more interested in watching their waistlines than in watching synchronized swimming? Answer: Take the toughest guys you could find (Dick

Butkus, John Madden, Rosey Grier) and let them do it for you. From 1973 to 1978, the Lite brand that was "everything you wanted in a beer—and less" featured over eighty commercials that actually made it cool to drink light beer (it didn't hurt that one of its subtly marketed attributes was the fact that you could drink a lot more of it than regular beer). When the argument between "tastes great" and "less filling" was finally over in 1978, Miller had gone from 7 million to 31 million barrels a year—the largest growth ever recorded in the history of brewing.

History

Fred Pabst wasn't the only German making beer in Milwaukee during the mid to late 1800s. Another Frederick was also getting himself established in the United States: Frederick Edward John Miller, the wealthy scion of a family of German businessmen. Sent to France for his education, Miller got more than seven years of school education; and thanks to his uncle, a respected brewer in France, Miller received a practical education in brewing, which he used to lease his first brewery, the brewery of the Hohenzollern royal family located in Sigmaringen, Germany. After several years of brewing the royal ale, political upheaval in Germany compelled Frederick to move his family to America and seek his fortune in Milwaukee, Wisconsin by purchasing the Plank Road Brewery from the Best family and turning it into the Miller Brewing Company in 1855.

Over the course of thirty-five years, Miller grew the company from a 300-barrel-a-year operation into a brewery capable of producing more than 75,000 barrels by 1888, the year he passed away. His sons took over his beer-making legacy. In 1903 the famous "High Life" brand was created, and Miller continued to prosper through the world wars, the Depression, and Prohibition. The brand remained a steady, albeit undistinguished, presence in the marketplace until 1970, when Phillip Morris purchased the company, giving it the financial clout to acquire other brands. Among them were Meister Bräu and its "Lite" label. By the time Americans had decided whether Lite beer "tasted great" or was "less filling," in the late '70s, Miller Brewing had taken the number two spot among national brewers.

SCHLITZ

THE CAN THAT OPENS LIKE A BEER BOTTLE

By: Jos. Schlitz Brewing Company (now Pabst Brewing Company)
Where: Milwaukee, WI
From: 1858–Present
Slogans: "The Beer That Made Milwaukee Famous"
       "Just the Kiss of the Hops"
Song: I drink Schlitz proud and strong / I could drink Schlitz all night long / So raise a glass to the time at hand / 'Cause Schlitz is the best beer in the land.

Overview

For younger aficionados who grew up in the era of Schlitz Malt Liquor Bull—a beer more closely associated with Billy Dee Williams than a historic German Beer Baron—it is difficult to appreciate the rich history of the brand. Today, "the beer that made Milwaukee famous" is largely relegated to the bottom of the beer cooler, where bargain-priced beverages can be found. However, I'll wager that there were more than a few dads out there who swore by Schlitz and wouldn't let a drop of Budweiser or Pabst pass their lips.

In the 1950s and 1960s, Schlitz was one of the top selling brands in America, earning its reputation—and a lot of loyal customers—due to large volume, good price, and plenty of national marketing.

History

Sometimes all it takes for success is fluency in math and a few disasters. Joseph Schlitz, the son of a German beer broker, found himself in a fortuitous position in 1856. Working as a bookkeeper for a Chestnut Street brewery in Milwaukee was a good start for Schlitz, but when the owner, August Krug, died, Schlitz married his widow and took over operations. Two years later, the Jos. Schlitz Brewery was officially born.

Another unfortunate event helped make Schlitz into one of the biggest brewers in Milwaukee: the Great Chicago Fire of 1871. The fire tainted Chicago's natural water supply to such an extent that Joseph was able to capitalize by offering thirsty Chicagoans something more substantial to drink: Schlitz beer. The steady southward flow of Schlitz into Chicago expanded its brand presence to the largest market in the Midwest. The slogan "the beer that made Milwaukee famous" can be directly attributed to this effort.

Unfortunately, the career that was born through misfortune ended similarly in 1875, when the *SS Schiller*, a cruise ship upon which Joseph booked passage for a European vacation, sank. Joseph perished, and the company's management passed over to August Krug's nephew, August Uihlein. Under the direction of Uihlein, Schlitz developed a large network of sales agents and its own railroad distribution system. It is estimated that, by 1907, the Uihlein family fortune was up to a hundred million dollars. Sales continued steadily up to Prohibition, when the company converted its manufacturing facilities to produce candy, among other products.

After Prohibition, Schlitz continued its meteoric rise, even briefly claiming the number one spot in American brewing production. It was consistently among the national brewing leaders until the late 1960s. Sadly, production problems due to an experimental fermentation process led to several batches of bad beer and the subsequent erosion of the brand's image, depressing sales. Eventually, Stroh's purchased Schlitz, ending its long reign as one of the leading American beer brands. Today, Schlitz is enjoying a small resurgence under beer marketer Pabst Brewing, who acquired Stroh Brewing.

Try it Yourself

Hold short pencil between first and second fingers as shown. Then without touching pencil with thumb or with object, move it to space between second and third fingers, to third and fourth fingers, finally back to original position, always pointing pencil outward.

Schlitz

THE BEER THAT MADE MILWAUKEE FAMOUS

Preferred... *for mellow moments*

HAMM'S

By: Theo. Hamm Brewing Company (now Miller Brewing Company)
Where: St. Paul, MN
From: 1864–Present
Slogan: "From the Land of Sky Blue Waters"
Song: From the land of sky blue waters (waters), / From the land of pines, lofty balsam, / Comes the beer refreshing, / Hamm's—the beer refreshing.

Overview

Long before Spuds McKenzie or the Budweiser frogs and lizards, Hamm's discovered one of the central tenets of beer marketing: animal mascots sell beer. The Hamm's bear began his career in 1953, and went on a nearly fifty-year run as the brand's chief spokesperson.

History

Theodore Hamm (1825-1903) came to St. Paul, Minnesota in 1856 looking to ply his trade as a butcher. A year later, the thirty-one-year-old Hamm changed his career, opening a small saloon. Seven years of on-the-job training convinced Hamm to get on the brewing side of the business and, in 1864, Hamm started his venerable brewery.

Hamm ran the business until 1891, when he stepped down from active management and let his son, William, take over. Under William's direction, Hamm Brewing grew into the state's leading brewer. Hamm's, always a smaller player on the national scene, reached its apex in terms of production in the mid-1960s, when it was the seventh largest producer in America. The 1970s saw Hamm's popularity fall amidst searing competition from mega-brewers Busch and Miller. In 1975, Hamm's was acquired by Olympia Brewing, ending its run as Minnesota's largest brewer. Hamm's is now produced by the Miller Brewing Company.

MICHELOB

By: Anheuser-Busch Brewing Company
Where: St. Louis, MO
From: 1896–Present
Slogans: "Weekends are made for Michelob."
"Who says you can't have it all?"

Overview

In the heady days of the 1970s, we were told that weekends were made for Michelob. Later on, we were encouraged to "put a little weekend in our week," suggesting that Michelob was not just for weekends anymore, but perhaps appropriate for several nights of the week as well—say, Thursday and Friday. In the mad 1980s Michelob encouraged us to really let our hair down; after all, "the night belonged to Michelob," and who were we to resist? By taking the wildly popular "this Bud's for you" concept up a notch, Anheuser-Busch made Michelob America's most popular special occasion beer—and its distinctive packaging and shapely bottle reinforced the idea that Michelob was not just some beer to swill down after a tough day at work, but rather the one you ordered after you showered and put a collared shirt on.

History

Michelob was America's first truly premium beer brand. The brand was created in 1896 when Budweiser founder Adolphus Busch traveled to Bohemia, tasted a beer he enjoyed, and bought the recipe. Slightly more refined than Budweiser, with a hoppier flavor and crisper aftertaste, unpasteurized Michelob found its niche in the domestic beer market as "fresh" beer, meant to be served exclusively on draught. Its high price and exclusive distribution (it accounted for only 4 percent of the brewer's total production in the 1950s) differentiated it from both Bud and the myriad of competitive beers on the market, and America's first truly "super premium" beer was born.

Back in the early twentieth century, Michelob sold for nearly five times the price of the typical lager and quickly earned a reputation for being "America's Highest Priced Draught Beer" (as was advertised in 1955). To heighten its premium allure, Anheuser-Busch created trendy packaging for the beer (Michelob's unique "lava lamp"–shaped bottle was such a breakthrough that it won several design awards at the time) that helped to raise sales and further cement the domestic super premium beer category. These days, Michelob Ultra is the leading Michelob brand, promising a reduced-carb drinking experience.

BALLANTINE

By: P. Ballantine & Sons (now Pabst Brewing Company)
Where: Albany, NY, and Newark, NJ
From: 1833–Present
Slogan: "Purity. Body. Flavor."
Song: Who is the Ale Man? / He could be you— / The man with the thirst for the manlier brew. / Three out of four men, every time, / Choose the coolest, clearest-tasting ale: / Ballantine.

Overview

Ballantine has been around since 1833, but it didn't reach its heyday until the late 1940s. Although not the largest producer (in 1950, Ballantine was third in production, behind Schlitz and Anheuser-Busch), Ballantine's unique style captured the American imagination through a clever marketing strategy that included both sports sponsorships and ads featuring famous American writers. Ernest Hemingway's only commercial endorsement in his whole life was a print ad for the beer:

FINCA VIGIA, SAN FRANCISCO DE PAULA, CUBA—
Bob Benchley first introduced me to Ballantine Ale. It has been a good companion ever since. You have to work hard to deserve to drink it. But I would rather have a bottle of Ballantine Ale than any other drink after fighting a really big fish. We keep it iced in the bait box with chunks of ice packed around it. And you ought to taste it on a hot day when you have worked a big marlin fast because there were sharks after him. You are tired all the way through. The fish is landed untouched by sharks and you have a bottle of Ballantine cold in your hand and drink it cool, light and full-bodied, so it tastes good long after you have swallowed it. That's the test of an ale with me: whether it tastes as good afterwards as when it's going down. Ballantine does.

Other writers, including John Steinbeck, did likewise. Not to mention super-celebrities of the time, including Marilyn Monroe, Joe DiMaggio, and Frank Sinatra. Between these high-profile celebrity endorsements and sponsorships of the Yankees, Phillies, and Boston Celtics (Ballantine owned the team for a short period), Ballantine is the 1950s equivalent of today's Stella Artois—a high volume beer with a premium, trendy reputation.

History

If German brewers created the great American lager, then it was a Scotsman, Peter Ballantine, who created the great American ale. Like his Bavarian colleagues, Ballantine came to America in 1820 with the intention of finding a better life for his family. He quickly found work in Albany at a brewery and eventually saved up enough money to open his own brewery there in 1833. Longing to be closer to a larger market, in 1840 Ballantine wisely selected Newark, New Jersey, as the site of his first large-scale production effort.

A quarter century later, New York's ever-expanding population and Ballantine's reputation for good quality ale put him in the top twenty producers in the nation—and the only ale among the group. Ballantine's symbol, the interlocking three-ring design representing "Purity, Body, Flavor" was inspired by three wet beer rings left on a bar as Peter Ballantine consumed a pint. The symbol—along with Ballantine's famous triple-X ("XXX") designation—still graces the necks of Ballantine's bottles today.

In 1972, Ballantine sold out to Falstaff for $4 million, ending the company's era of independence. Falstaff remained true to the formula, however, and even improved upon the beer by introducing the famous "puzzle caps," featuring a series of clever rebus cryptographs (whose difficulty seems to increase in tandem with one's consumption of the ale). Pabst acquired Ballantine in the Falstaff takeover in the early 1990s and still brews it today.

IRON CITY

By: Iron City Brewery (now Pittsburgh Brewing Company)
Where: Pittsburgh, PA
From: 1861–Present
Slogans: "The Beer Drinker's Beer"
"A Tradition of Brewing Excellence"

Overview

Even if you've never set foot in Pittsburgh, you have to give credit to Pittsburgh Brewing Company for two of the greatest marketing innovations in the history of beer: the 1962 invention of the "snap-top" self-opening can (with Alcoa), and the creation of the sports souvenir can. The first enabled easy access to your beer—prior to the snap top, you had to employ the fabled "church key," or can opener. The second enabled Pittsburgh fans to gaze into the graceful countenance of Franco Harris while sipping a can of Iron City.

History

Iron City Brewery (along with Iron City Beer) was founded in 1861 in Pittsburgh by Edward Frauenheim, a young German immigrant. In eight years, Frauenheim grew the brewery from a one vat setup to a burgeoning operation spanning three facilities.

In 1899, Iron City Brewery merged with twenty other regional breweries to form the Pittsburgh Brewing Company, a behemoth with a combined annual capacity of a million barrels. The move allowed it to weather the twin storms of war and Prohibition. It was one of the few breweries to emerge from Prohibition and continued to flourish as a solid regional player for many years after.

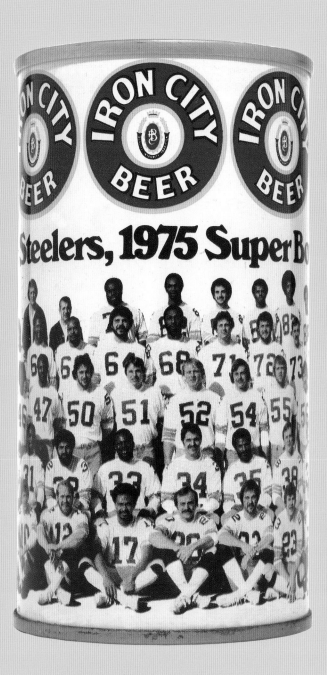

SCHAEFER

By: F. & M. Schaefer Brewing Company
    (now Pabst Brewing Company)
Where: New York, NY
From: 1842–Present
Slogans: "(Schaefer is the one beer to have) When
        you're having more than one."
      "America's Oldest Lager Beer"
Song: Schaefer's flavor /Doesn't fade / Even when your
    thirst is done. / The most rewarding flavor /In this
    man's world / For people who are having fun . . . /
    Schaefer is the / One beer to have / When you're
    having more than one!

Overview

Many agree that there is no finer achievement in advertising than BBD&O's 1961 creation of the Schaefer jingle: "Schaefer is the one beer to have when you're having more than one." Nowadays, the very notion expressed in that simple ad would be enough to draw a boycott, and perhaps a lawsuit. In 1961, however, it was generally assumed that whenever a beer drinker started drinking, he would have at least two or, perhaps, even six beers.

There is something to be said for "knowing your customer." Beer drinkers—especially those in New York and the surrounding tri-state area—had much "more than one" and subsequently made Schaefer one of the most popular beers in the country, prompting expansion to several plants throughout the northeast in the 1960s and '70s.

History

The story of the longest-running major brewery in New York City follows a familiar theme. Take one young German immigrant and his brother, some yeast from the old country, give him a job and a savings account, and—presto—a great American beer is born. Thus, in a nutshell, is the story of the F. & M. Schaefer Brewing Company, founded in 1842 by brothers Frederick and Maximillian Schaefer. New Yorkers immediately took

a liking to the brothers' uniquely-styled lager (what beer *didn't* they like, back then?), and the operation was forced to move to larger and larger facilities. In fact, the company's continuous relocation may have played an equally important role in its success as its brewing formula; every time the factory moved, the price of the real estate it sat upon had rocketed sky high. (Schaefer Brewing once occupied and owned a good chunk of the prime real estate around New York's Grand Central Station.)

Eventually, the company settled in Brooklyn, where it brewed beer until 1976. The real heyday of Schaefer was the 1950s, when it went on an acquisition spree, purchasing plants in Cleveland, Albany, and Baltimore in order to ramp up production. Eventually, the company decided to build an ultra-modern facility in Lehigh Valley, Pennsylvania, and closed New York City's longest operating brewery. For many New Yorkers, Schaefer was no longer "the one beer to have." In 1981, the company was sold to Stroh's. Stroh's was sold to Pabst Brewing in 1999, which still brews Schaefer today.

RHEINGOLD

Enjoy yourself!
It's a
Rheingold Day!
Rheingold
EXTRA DRY
Rheingold Breweries, Inc.
Orange, N.J. and New Bedford, Mass.
#33

By: Leibman Breweries (now Rheingold Brewing Company)
Where: Brooklyn, NY
From: 1883–Present
Slogans: "It's beer as beer *should* taste!"
"*Always* refreshing—*never* filling!"
Song: My beer is Rheingold, the dry beer. / Think of Rheingold whenever you buy beer . . . / It's not bitter, not sweet, it's the dry flavored treat. / Won't you try EXTRA DRY Rheingold beer?

Overview

1977 was a tough time to be a New Yorker. With the exception of the Yankees winning the World Series, 1977 featured the serial killings of the self-styled "Son of Sam," the burning of the Bronx, a major blackout (followed by light rioting), and the end of Rheingold, the city's favorite beer. To some of the 4,000 brewery workers who got laid off, the wounds still seem fresh today. Ask a native New Yorker older than fifty to sing you the Rheingold jingle ("My beer is Rheingold, the dry beer"), and you won't be disappointed. Such was the impact Rheingold had on New York.

Luckily, Walter "Terry" Liebman (a descendant of the founding family, who worked at Rheingold until 1961) brought the beer back to life in 1999. Brewed at Greenpoint Beer Works in Brooklyn, Rheingold is helping to bring back a tradition that started in the late 1800s, when Brooklyn's hundred-plus breweries made more beer than Milwaukee and Detroit combined.

Now Rheingold is a "hip" and "trendy" beer, more likely to be seen in the hand of a tattooed youngster from the East Village than a tattooed construction worker from Bensonhurst. The price has also gone up significantly (in some New York delis, it's more expensive than imported brands). However, that classic "dry" taste remains the same, as does the classically styled bottle.

History

As the story goes, the Rheingold brand name was inspired by a comment made by the conductor of the Metropolitan Opera in 1883. Eyeing the golden color of the beer, he remarked that it was the color of "Rheingold," referring to Germany's great river. Thus, a New York legend was born. Fortunate circumstances extended the company's reach in 1895, when Sadie Liebman (granddaughter of the founder Joseph Liebman) married Samuel Simon Steiner, a leading hops trader. Production and quality grew accordingly, until the company was producing upwards of 700,000 barrels a year by 1914.

Although Rheingold was another beer in the stalwart tradition of the German masters, it will be remembered more for its cutting-edge marketing approach than its "extra dry" finish. After suffering through the world wars and Prohibition, Rheingold entered its golden era. Starting in 1942, Rheingold's female spokesmodel, Miss Rheingold, began to be selected by vote. The annual contest to crown the new Miss Rheingold was a New York tradition that captured the public's imagination to an extent that surpassed even the company's wildest expectations. In 1959 (according to corporate lore) an estimated 22 million votes were cast in the Miss Rheingold contest. Presidential election tallies were the only larger vote ever recorded.

BLATZ

By: Blatz Brewing (now Pabst Brewing Company)
Where: Milwaukee, WI
From: 1851–Present
Slogans: "Milwaukee's *First* Bottled Beer"
"Milwaukee's *Finest* Beer!"
Song: I'm from Milwaukee, and I ought to know. / It's draft brewed Blatz beer, wherever you go. / Smoother, and fresher, less filling, that's clear. . . . / Blatz is Milwaukee's finest beer!

Overview

In 1951, Blatz played an instrumental role in the new television advertising revolution by becoming the sole sponsor of what beer author Carl Miller describes as "television's first major 'media event'," the switch from radio to television of the popular *Amos & Andy* show. The move solidified Blatz's reputation as one of the leading American beer brands.

How times change. A generation later, Blatz was the poster child of "cheap beer" (in 1986, a case sold for as little as seven dollars in parts of the country). Today, it is still one of America's leading "value" brands. Despite its current status, Blatz has a proud Milwaukee heritage that started back in 1851, when Valentin Blatz acquired Milwaukee's City Brewery. It was also the first of the Milwaukee beers to go national, beating both Pabst and Anheuser-Busch to the punch.

History

Blatz was founded in 1851 by the time-honored tradition of marrying the boss's widow. Valentin Blatz basically learned the brewing trade from his boss at Milwaukee City Brewery, Bavarian beer master John Braun, and took over his brewery (and his wife) when he died. The brewery quickly earned a reputation for its solid lager-style beer, and was incorporated in 1889 as the Val Blatz Brewing Company. Two years later, Blatz sold out to a group of London financiers known as "the English syndicate." The brand prospered throughout the early to mid twentieth century, reaching its height in the early 1950s, when Blatz print ads featured celebrities such as Groucho Marx touting their allegiance to Blatz by stating, "I've been to Milwaukee— I ought to know ... that Blatz is Milwaukee's *Finest* Beer!"

Despite its rich heritage and attempts to modernize the brand through advertising, Blatz couldn't keep up with the majors and closed in 1959. The brand was sold to Pabst, who sold it to G. Heileman a decade later. Pabst Brewing eventually reclaimed the brand through its acquisition of Stroh's and continues to brew it today.

Your face will light up, too!

JUST the *sight* of a sparkling glass of Blatz Beer puts a big smile on thirsty folks' faces. And Blatz *tastes* as refreshing as it looks, for this grand old Milwaukee brew has been mellowed to the very peak of flavor. For 96 years, we've brewed Blatz *only in*

Milwaukee . . . home of America's finest beers . . . and we're pleased to say that Blatz is Milwaukee's *first* bottled beer. If you can't get Blatz, please be patient. We're growing as fast as good building and good brewing will let us, to bring Blatz to your neighborhood—soon.

Milwaukee's first ... America's finest ... Bottled beer

Blatz BREWING BETTER BEER FOR THE 96TH YEAR

FALSTAFF

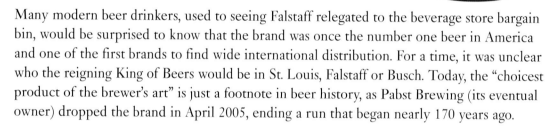

By: Falstaff Brewing Company
Where: St. Louis, MO
From: 1870–2005
Slogans: "The Choicest Product of the Brewer's Art"
         "America's Premium Quality Beer"

Overview

Many modern beer drinkers, used to seeing Falstaff relegated to the beverage store bargain bin, would be surprised to know that the brand was once the number one beer in America and one of the first brands to find wide international distribution. For a time, it was unclear who the reigning King of Beers would be in St. Louis, Falstaff or Busch. Today, the "choicest product of the brewer's art" is just a footnote in beer history, as Pabst Brewing (its eventual owner) dropped the brand in April 2005, ending a run that began nearly 170 years ago.

History

Although the Falstaff brand name wasn't trademarked until 1903 (the owner thought the Shakespearean character's intelligence and fondness for drink represented the type of "smart drinker" that would thwart the temperance movement's mischaracterization of alcohol users), and the brewery wasn't "officially" founded until 1870, Falstaff beer goes way back to 1838. That was the year that Johann Adam Lemp, a German immigrant, started brewing beer in his St. Louis grocery store. Lemp's lager beer soon took hold among the steadily increasing immigrant population, and another Beer Baron was born.

By the time Adam Lemp died in 1862, his brand was the biggest of forty in St. Louis, and his son William was firmly established in the business. By 1879, Falstaff was the tenth largest brewer in America (over Anheuser-Busch) and, by 1890, it was the first beer to go national. Despite the fierce rivalry between the two master brewers, Lemp joined forces with Adolphus Busch to start the Galveston Brewing Company (which Falstaff would later buy outright). Lemp's predilection for mergers didn't end with his deal with Busch, however; the 1897 marriage of his daughter Hilda to Pabst heir Gustav united the two largest brewing families of the day. Sadly, the death of Lemp's close friend, Captain Frederick Pabst, was the event that finally drove William Lemp to commit suicide in 1904, starting a spiral of bad events that would eventually force the company to close in 1918.

In 1920, the year after Prohibition started, the Lemp family sold the Falstaff name to Joseph "Papa Joe" Griesedieck, a small local brewer. The company stayed afloat by selling near-beer and cured hams. By 1933, when Prohibition ended, the company re-entered the business officially as the Falstaff Brewing Company.

The next several decades saw a period of expansion in which Falstaff purchased breweries in Omaha, New Orleans, Galveston, El Paso, Fort Wayne, San Francisco, and Cranston, Rhode Island. By the mid 1960s, Falstaff was the third largest brewer in the nation, with sales of nearly 5 million barrels. At one time or another, Falstaff Brewing was the owner of Narragansett, Lucky Lager, Ballantine, and Munich Beer, among others.

But by 1975, the company was riddled with debt and going through a series of plant closings. Ten years later, the writing was plainly on the wall, when the company turned to producing novelty beers such as "M*A*S*H 4077" beer and the infamous white cans of generic "beer" (whose slogan was the clever "Beer: just ask for it by name"). By 1990, the company's last remaining plant in Fort Wayne was shuttered.

Pabst took over the brand in the early 1990s and continued to brew it until 2005, when low sales forced the famous Falstaff out of business.

PIELS

By: Piel Brothers Brewery (now Pabst Brewing Company)
Where: Brooklyn, NY
From: 1883–Present
Slogans: "The Beer Drinker's Beer"
"The Kind of Beer You First Loved"

Overview

Piels's greatest contribution to beer was the concept of "real draft" beer in a can. In 1966, Piels came out with a filtered, non-pasteurized beer in a can, beating Miller's "genuine draft" to the punch by a few decades. Of course, old-time New Yorkers remember Piels as a true New York staple from 1955 to 1960 (and later, in 1975), when the legendary "Bert and Harry" characters were the animated spokesmen for the brand. At the height of their popularity, Bert and Harry had more than 100,000 people enrolled in their own fan club.

History

The Piel Brothers Brewery was founded in 1883 by Gottfried, Michael, and Wilhelm Piel of Düsseldorf, Germany. By 1911, the brewery that had started out brewing less than 1,000 barrels a year was spitting out over 40,000 barrels, and the name "Piels" was synonymous with New York beer. Although Prohibition took some steam out of their sales, the brothers plunked down $1,000,000 to ramp the plant up to 400,000 barrel-a-year capacity in 1933. By 1948, production had doubled, and the famous "Bert and Harry" burst onto the scene just a few years later—cementing the brand as one of New York's favorites.

BLACK LABEL

By: W&J Carling Company (now Pabst Brewing Company)
Where: London, Ontario (Canada)
From: 1840–Present
Slogans: "Mabel, Black Label"
         "America's Lusty, Lively Beer!"

Overview

What do Pamela Anderson, John Candy, and Carling's Black Label beer have in common? They are all Canadians who achieved their fame and fortune in America. Although Carling was founded in Canada, it didn't take long for the company to come to the United States—and thank God it did.

Long before Budweiser came out with its "Born On" marketing program, which dated each beer can's date of manufacture, Carling was using freshness as a selling tool. After acquiring Illinois's Stag Brewery, Hyde Park Brewery in St. Louis, and Michigan's Frankenmuth Brewery (among others) in the mid to late 1950s, Carling had a national network of breweries and marketed their fresh beer approach with a continental map showing all of the Carling locations. It took about five years of acquisition and double-digit growth to take Carling from a local favorite to a great American beer.

History

Although most Americans would assume Black Label is a 100 percent American product, the beer got its start in London, Ontario, way back in 1818. Local legend has it that Thomas Carling (a transplant from England) got his start by brewing beer for the gentlemen who helped him clear his fields of tree stumps. A lot of land clearing was going on back then, and the tradition was for every neighbor to chip in with some oxen and back-breaking work to help a new farmer get started. Invariably, it was Carling's beer that was served at these neighborhood "stumping bees," as they were called. His success among his neighbors eventually encouraged him to start his own brewery in 1840, giving birth to the Carling Brewery.

Carling's move into the States didn't happen until more than a century later, when the repeal of Prohibition and a failing car company came together to create American beer history. Peerless Motor Cars were high-end vehicles and a bit too nice for Depression-era wallets, so the company was looking to switch industries. It eyed one that in 1933 seemed to offer unlimited growth potential: beer. For 25,000 shares of stock, Carling sold the rights to their beer and Canadians came down to the States to convert a car factory into a brewery. The experiment worked, and Black Label was born.

The brand waxed and waned until about 1950, when the famous "Mabel" character was introduced. First played by actress Jeanne Goodspeed, Mabel—a sassy barmaid permanently attached to a tray full of Black Label (every man's fantasy)—captured America's imagination and propelled Black Label to yearly double-digit sales growth for the next decade. A series of acquisitions in the '50s and '60s kept Carling at the forefront, as they added brands such as Stag and Heidelburg to their roster.

By the 1970s, the Anheuser-Busch and Miller behemoths were rolling over Carling, and the company went into a steady decline until 1979, when the company was purchased by G. Heileman, which was purchased by Stroh's, which was bought by Pabst, which makes Black Label under contract to this day.

COORS

By: Coors Brewing Company
Where: Golden, CO
From: 1873–Present
Slogan: "The Taste of the Rockies"

Overview

For those of us in the Northeast back in the 1970s, Coors beer was the beer lover's Cuban cigar: illegal, mysterious, and highly desirable. In 1977, when the film *Smokey and the Bandit* came out, this reputation was engraved in stone. In the film, the Bandit (played by Burt Reynolds) agrees to the sum of $80,000 to transport 400 cases of Coors from Texarkana to Atlanta. The road is fraught with danger (and dangerous performances, including Jackie Gleason's portrayal of Sheriff Buford T. Justice), but the Bandit, aided by his 1977 Pontiac Trans Am, pulls through. All I could think of was that the Coors cost that Atlanta businessman $400 a case! At that time, unpasteurized Coors was only sold in eleven western states (the company didn't believe the beer would ship well and limited its distribution to the western side of the Mississippi, though it was never technically illegal)—thus was the "Coors mystique" born.

Well, the legend was tastier than reality. Coors is a great beer, but certainly not worth $400 a case. However, with rumors that President Ford exclusively stocked it on Air Force One and celebrities like Paul Newman who swore by it, the Coors legend grew. Today, the brand is better known for its "Silver Bullet" light beer and the attendant bikini-clad models that advertise it. Still, the "taste of the Rockies" is the same as it was back in the 1970s, when it was as elusive to Northeasterners as a Cuban cigar.

History

Adolph Coors was born in 1847, about a hundred years before anyone would take issue with his given name. After eighth grade, he spent a six-year stint apprenticing in a German brewery, and then—like so many others before him—took his newfound knowledge to America, where he could earn a living. His 1868 trek eventually took him to the Midwest—but not before he was caught stowing away on the ship that brought him and was forced to find a job in Baltimore to pay off his debt. He eventually got to Illinois, where he found employment with the Stenger Brewery for three years. Seeing the potential in young Adolph, Stenger continually encouraged Coors to court his daughters. A love connection was never made, however, and Adolph fled under duress to greener pastures free from the threat of matrimony. He ended up in Denver, a city then only fourteen years old.

Spying his entry into the beer business, Coors purchased a fledgling bottling business with the money he had saved at Stenger's and by 1873 was doing a brisk business selling beer, cider, and seltzer water. In the meantime, he spent weekends searching the Denver foothills for a water source for his dream. In Golden, he found an abundant supply of water for his brewery and, back in Denver, he found Jacob Schuler, an abundant supply of money. Adolph sold the bottling company and partnered up with Schuler to create the Golden Brewery. The resulting product, "Golden Lager," became an instant success in Denver and has been the beer of the West ever since.

Today, Coors has the distinction of owning the largest single-site brewery in the world. Coors also owns the Coors Brewers Ltd., which manufactures the UK version of Carling. In 1959, Coors also became the first brewer to use an all-aluminum can, a revolution that changed the industry and created the recycling craze. The can company Coors helped establish now produces over 4 billion—yes, *billion*—cans annually. It's a good thing they invented recycling.

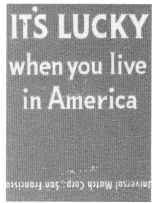

The Great
American Beers

LÖWENBRÄU

By: Miller Brewing Company
Where: Milwaukee, WI
From: 1975–1999
Slogan: "Let it be Löwenbräu."
Song: Here's to good friends. / Tonight is kind of special . . . /
The beer we'll pour / Must be something more (somehow). / So
tonight . . . tonight . . . / Let it be Löwenbräu.

I go wild as I sip from a cold Löwenbräu.
—*lyric from "Brothers on My Jock" EPMD, sung by Redman*

With Anheuser-Busch's popular Michelob premium beer winning over consumers' palates in the 1970s, Miller Brewing had to strike back. Their answer? Take a legendary Bavarian beer with nearly 600 years of history and reformulate it for the American market. Thus, Löwenbräu, Miller's super-premium beer, was born in Milwaukee in 1975, eventually becoming America's number one super premium beer. The beer ultimately went back to Europe, where it is brewed by the Spaten-Löwenbräu group under its original formulation.

One of the best things to come from Miller's largely unsuccessful experiment with Löwenbräu was the knowledge that big breweries do best when they stick to what they know: making lots of lager beer. The failure of Big Brewing to capture the craft beer fan's critical acclaim helped spark the small beer movement, which continues to do what it is best at: giving consumers lots of new regional beer to choose from. When Miller left its license to brew Löwenbräu on the table and went back to focusing on brewing High Life and Lite beer, everybody won (except Löwenbräu fans, like me—but we'll survive).

KNICKERBOCKER

By: Jacob Ruppert Brewing
Where: New York, NY
From: 1867–1995
Slogan: "Satisfies Your Beer Thirst Better!"

Even though not one golden sip of Knickerbocker beer has ever passed my lips, I can tell you for a fact that it is one of my favorite beers of all time. There are two reasons. First, because I admire any non-military man that can get people to call him "The Colonel," and second—and more important—Knickerbocker beer built the greatest baseball stadium in the world: Yankee Stadium. From all historical accounts, it also seems to have been a pretty decent tasting beer.

The man that put it all together in early New York was none other than "Colonel" Jacob Ruppert, a Beer Baron like no other. Starting at his father's Turtle Bay Brewery at the age of ten, Jacob Ruppert saw beer as his ticket to a better life.

Ruppert's Extra Pale Ale and Knickerbocker soon dominated beer sales in New York, and Ruppert, ever the savvy operator, widened his circle to become a business with local and national political ties. A social butterfly, his honorary "Colonel" title (bestowed upon him by then-Governor Hill) didn't hurt his standing among New York's elite, who liberally tolerated his flamboyance. Sensing a good outlet for his Ruppert beer, the Colonel purchased the Yankees in 1914 and was instrumental in the acquisition of Babe Ruth from the Boston Red Sox—a move that began a downturn for the Boston franchise that lasted until 2004, when the Sox snapped an eighty-six-year losing streak to win the World Series.

GRAIN BELT

By: Minneapolis Brewing Company (now August Schell Brewery)
Where: New Ulm, MN
From: 1893–Present
Slogans: "The Friendly Beer with the Friendly Flavor"
"It's Been a Long Time a-Brewin'"

Grain Belt's real slogan should be "the beer they couldn't kill." Launched in 1893 by the Minneapolis Brewing Company, Grain Belt beer quickly became a bestseller in, well, America's Midwestern grain belt. The beer sold well until 1920, when Prohibition killed it for the first time. After Prohibition, Grain Belt reemerged as "the friendly beer with the friendly flavor" and prospered until well into the 1960s, when it was the top seller in its home state of Minnesota. To reflect the brand's importance, the brewery was renamed "Grain Belt Breweries" and continued churning out the popular Grain Belt Golden and Grain Belt Premium beers until 1976, when G. Heileman acquired the company after several years of lackluster sales in the face of stiff competition from Miller and Anheuser-Busch.

At Heileman, GB played third fiddle to brands Old Style and Schmidt and eventually became the company's most heavily discounted brand, and quality suffered. By the 1980s, Heileman was having problems of its own and was forced to sell the old Schmidt brewery (where Grain Belt was produced) and the brands to the newly formed Minnesota Brewing Company. The company improved the quality, and sales of GB were back on track once again. That lasted until 2002, when Minnesota Brewing went under—but not Grain Belt! Old GB found new owners, August Schell Brewing, and moved back to New Ulm, the ancestral home of Grain Belt's founders, where it is still brewed today.

STROH'S

By: Lion Brewery (now Pabst Brewing Company)
Where: Detroit, MI
From: 1850–Present
Slogans: "Served Whenever Quality Counts"
"America's Fire-Brewed Beer"

In my mind, Stroh's is one of the preeminent American beers for one simple reason: the thirty-pack. There is just something comforting about having those extra six beers, and, at the very least, Stroh's should be commended for adopting this glorious packaging tactic.

In 1850 Bernhard Stroh arrived in Detroit, Michigan, after two years spent fleeing the German Revolution of 1848. Formally trained as a brewer, Stroh quickly opened up the Lion Brewery and began selling his unique brand of light lager door-to-door from an applecart. By the time he passed away in 1882, his beer business was strong enough to survive his death, and his sons Julius and Bernhard, Jr., continued the legacy, eventually renaming the brewery Stroh Brewery in 1902.

Stroh is perhaps best remembered for its famous "Stroh's Bohemian" beer, a Detroit staple since 1850. A longtime regional brewer, Stroh ramped up its production over the twentieth century, eventually going on an acquisitive spate beginning in 1980. Stroh developed a portfolio of some of the greatest American brands ever made, including Lone Star, Schaefer, Schlitz, Old Style, Old Milwaukee, Schmidt's, Mickey's, Black Label, Blatz, Red White & Blue, Henry Weinhard's—and even everybody's favorite malt liquor, Colt 45.

Ultimately, the acquisitions were difficult to digest, and Anheuser-Busch, Miller, and Coors were too strong to compete with. In 1990, Stroh sold the brands to Pabst and Miller, and a proud Detroit tradition ended. However, Pabst still brews Stroh's to this day.

OLYMPIA

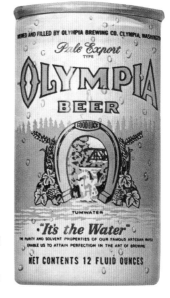

By: Olympia Brewing Company
      (now Pabst Brewing Company)
Where: Olympia, WA
From: 1896–Present
Slogans: "It's the Water!"
           "Perfection in the Art of Brewing"

"It's the water" is the classic American beer drinker's joke. Long derided by Europeans for our "thin, watery" American beer, Olympia's historic slogan almost taunts beer snobs to assess this noble lager solely on its merits. The water referenced on the can comes from artesian wells around Tumwater, Washington, site of the original brewery. Back in 1896, when Leopold Schmidt founded the Olympia Brewing Company and the Olympia brand, the marketing watchword of the day was water—the better the water, the better the brew. When taste buds matured as imports and microbrewing grew, the beer made famous for its water was heralding its American style to its disadvantage. Olympia is one of the founding fathers of beer in the American West, and Schmidt's legacy lasted until 1993, when the Tumwater plant (then producing about a third of the volume of a typical Miller plant) was closed, ending a century-old Washington brewing tradition.

Olympia, which has been brewed under contract by Pabst Brewing since its acquisition in 1983, will continue to be "the water," although not in Washington State. Sadly, Washington has no more high-volume breweries; its largest is now Redhook Ale Brewery, a small producer of microbrews.

RAINIER

By: Bay View Brewery (now Pabst Brewing Company)
Where: Seattle, WA
From: 1883–Present
Slogan: "Mountain Fresh Taste"

The beer we know today as Rainier was created in 1883, when John Kopp and Andrew Hemrich started what became the Bay View Brewery (and eventually the Rainier Brewing Company). Eleven years later, Bay View merged with the nearby Claussen-Sweeny Brewery and the Albert Braun Brewing Company to form the Seattle Brewing and Malting Company. By the turn of the century, the brewer, based in the Georgetown neighborhood of Seattle, was not only the largest on the west coast, but Washington State's largest industrial establishment. Their number-one product was Rainier beer.

Much has changed in the last century. In fact, just a few short months after winning the gold medal for best American pilsner at the Great American Beer Festival in 1998, the Rainier Brewery was put up for sale. Sold in 1999 to Stroh's, and then to Pabst, the famous Rainier Brewery (its giant neon "R" standing high above the south end of town) closed down for good, ending its 116-year run as a Seattle institution.

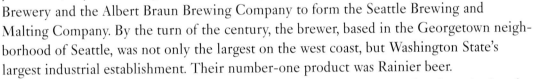

Under Pabst's management, the beer is starting to see an upturn in sales after multiple years of declining market share—largely due to the craze for everything retro. The old Rainier motorcycle ads—featuring a buzzing bike whining up Mount Rainier (buzzing "Raaaaaiineeeeer Beeeeeeer") are back—and the younger crowd is starting to embrace the brand again. The beer is now contract brewed for Pabst by Miller Brewing Company.

GENESEE CREAM ALE

Famous 12 horse ale

By: Genesee Brewing Company (now High Falls Brewing Company)
Where: Rochester, NY
From: 1878–Present
Slogan: "Real. Good. Beer."
Song: Genny cream, Genny cream / Never gives your taste a fight,
'Cause it's bold . . . without the bite / Bold . . . without the bite

With the preponderance of Genesee and Genesee Cream Ale in the state, it is hard to meet a New Yorker who doesn't have a strong opinion of the brand (for better or worse). The unique flavor of Genesee is partly attributed to "kraeusening," a traditional German brewmaking process whereby a small dosage of unfermented malt sugars (or "wort") is added to the conditioning tank. This secondary fermentation adds additional carbonation to the beer, leading to a smooth, "clean" aftertaste. A hefty dose of barley malt and quality hops make Genesee's beers distinct in flavor. Perhaps that is what distinguishes their famous "Genny Cream Ale," a beer that confounds many first-time imbibers; it seems to impart almost no "creamy" character whatsoever.

Since its founding in 1878 in Rochester, the Genesee Brewing Company has held the distinction of being America's largest regional brewer. Although its trademark 12 Horse Ale headed its product lineup for years, the company is most closely associated with its famous Cream Ale. High Falls Brewery, now the country's fifth largest brewer, purchased Genesee Brewing in 1990 and continues to brew Genesee and Genesee Cream Ale today.

the bright! taste in beer!
GENESEE
Beer
5-3 THE GENESEE BREWING CO., INC. • Rochester, N. Y.

LONE STAR

By: Lone Star Brewing Company (now Pabst Brewing Company)
Where: San Antonio, TX
From: 1940–Present
Slogan: "The National Beer of Texas"

From deep within the caverns of the Edwards aquifer comes the crystal-clear water that's helped make Lone Star the beer Texans call their own. Its smooth award-winning taste is carefully crafted and controlled to give you the consistent, drinkable brew you'd expect from The National Beer of Texas.

—Lone Star manifesto

Whenever I think of Lone Star beer I picture that scene from the *Blues Brothers* when the band, attempting to win over a honky-tonk crowd with blues covers, gets pelted by a steady stream of tall-necked beer bottles from behind the chicken-wire-covered stage. Lone Star is the kind of beer that needs to be had in Texas-sized portions and also in the correct atmosphere—whether it be a county music bar, the back of a Ford F-150, or at a high school football game. Locally, the jury is out on which Texas beer has truly become the official beer of Texas, however. San Antonio–based brews Pearl and Shiner also claim the allegiance of true Texans.

Built in 1884 by Adolphus Busch and a few savvy San Antonio businessmen, the Lone Star Brewery was the first mechanized brewery in Texas. From its founding to 1939, the brewery produced both Sabinas beer and Champion beer. In 1940, the "Champion" brand was reformulated and renamed Lone Star, and the "National Beer of Texas" was born. In 1976, Lone Star became a subsidiary of Olympia, eventually fell into the hands of the G. Heileman house and, subsequently, Pabst Brewing, under whose banner it is now brewed.

PEARL

By: Pearl Brewing Company (now Pabst Brewing Compan[y])
Where: San Antonio, TX
From: 1886–Present
Slogan: "First in the Heart of Texas"
"From the Country of 1,100 Springs"

Ask a Texan which beer he prefers, Pearl, Lone Star, or Shine[r] and he will most likely tell you that he likes "whichever is col[d]est." In terms of history, Pearl gets the edge by decades, makin[g] "first in the heart of Texas."

Started in 1881 in San Antonio as the J. B. Behloradsky Bre[w]ery, Pearl Brewing Company was purchased in 1883 by a group of San Antonio businessmen grouped under the banner of the San Antonio Brewing Association. Renamed the San Antonio Brewing Company, the brewery gave birth to Pearl Beer in 1886. According to company history, the "Pearl" name came from a German brewmaster who, gazing into a glass of the newly created lager, remarked that the bubbles resembled tiny "Perlen," or pearls. The beer's solid taste won over the local population, and, by 1916, San Antonio Brewing was the biggest brewery in the state. In 1952, the company changed its name to Pearl Brewing and began steadily acquiring smaller operations until the early 1980s. By that time, Pearl was available in nearly all of the fifty states. Perhaps the greatest moment for Pearl came in 1998 when, through the acquisition of Stroh's, longtime rival Lone Star was brought under the Pearl umbrella. Sadly, the year 2001 saw the closure of the Pearl brewery. The brands are now produced by Miller's Fort Worth plant under contract for Pabst.

SHINER

By: Spoetzl Brewery
Where: Shiner, TX
From: 1909–Present
Slogan: "Specially brewed for the discriminating beer drinker by the little brewery in Shiner."

Founded roughly a quarter century after the breweries that produce Lone Star and Pearl, Shiner has made up for lost time, using its retro styling and small-brand appeal to position itself as the hippest Texas beer export. With a population just a tad over 4,000 in 2000, with well over 50 percent of residents claiming Czech or German ancestry, Shiner is a small place where beer is big. In fact, the town of Shiner was settled in 1887 by Czech and German farmers, and it only took them until 1909 to form the Shiner Brewing Association, which later became the Spoetzl Brewery.

The Shiner Brewing Association was founded by a group of Texas businessmen, led by brewmaster Herman Weis, a brewer from Galveston. After a few years, the operation was taken over by Kosmos Spoetzl, a German brewer who had spent the past eight years working in an Egyptian brewery, and the Spoetzl Brewery was born.

Spoetzl's Bavarian-style beer was no easy sell at first—the brewer found himself driving around the Shiner countryside selling iced keg beer to sweaty farmers from the back of a Model T Ford. Eventually, the beer caught on. A brief hiatus on account of Prohibition merely stalled things for a while, and the Spoetzl Brewery opened again the minute after it ended, selling its beer on a strictly local basis. Spoetzl worked right up until 1950 when he died, leaving the business to his daughter Cecilie—one of the only female brewery owners in American history, and the only female owner at the time.

SCHMIDT'S

By: C. Schmidt & Sons Brewing Company
Where: Philadelphia, PA
From: 1859–1987
Slogans: "Beer as Beer Should Be"
"One Beautiful Beer"

In April 2005, Don Russell's exceptional "Joe Sixpack" column in the *Philadelphia Inquirer* covered the amazing and improbable story of the city's greatest beer taste test. The year was 1975 and a Philadelphia beer distributor named Piel Bros. had just figured out how to sell Coors on the East Coast by exploiting a loophole to get around the company's restriction on sales east of the Mississippi River. Soon, Philadelphia was awash in trendy and mysterious Coors beer, and Piel Bros. was selling over 4,000 cases a week. The sudden takeover of the Philadelphia market by a Colorado brewer loomed as a dark cloud over a proud Pennsylvania brewing history extending back more than three centuries.

The question was, "Just how good is Coors, anyway?" *Inquirer* food editor Bill Collins hastily assembled six other editors with beer drinking experience and set out to rate ten beers on a scale of one to ten. Coors finished squarely in the middle of the pack.

Where did Schmidt's come out? You guessed it. Number one. The surprising results held off the pending sale of the brewery to G. Heileman until 1987. The sale to Heileman ended a Philadelphia tradition that began in 1859, when the fledgling C. Schmidt & Sons Brewing Company pumped out 500 barrels of ale and porter. Schmidt's managed to survive Prohibition and attacks from Anheuser-Busch and Miller. While numerous brand acquisitions over the years kept the company in the game, the brewery will always be known for its hometown favorite, Schmidt's.

ROLLING ROCK

By: Latrobe Brewing Company
Where: Latrobe, PA
From: 1939–Present
Slogan: "33"

Rolling Rock. From the glass-lined tanks of Old Latrobe, we tender this premium beer for your enjoyment, as a tribute to your good taste. It comes from the mountain springs to you.

—Rolling Rock Pledge

The Latrobe Brewing Company was founded at the foot of Pennsylvania's Allegheny Mountains in 1893. The brewery went about its business unmolested for nearly thirty years until Prohibition closed its doors. In 1933, as soon as it was legal to do so, the brothers Frank, Joseph, Robert, Ralph, and Anthony Tito bought the brewing company lock, stock, and barrel and resumed the Rolling Rock tradition, which still flourishes today.

Of course, part of the Rolling Rock appeal has to do with the mysterious "33" printed on every can and bottle. According to the company, "33" may represent 1933, the year Prohibition was repealed, and/or the number of words in the Rolling Rock Pledge (see above). The truth is actually somewhere in between. According to former Latrobe Brewing CEO James Tito, there was some internal bickering over the company's slogan in 1939, the year the brand was started. The writer created the current "pledge," counted the words, and scribbled a big "33" on top of the paper and sent it to the bottler—who printed several million labels with the "33" notation still above the pledge. The company decided to keep the misprinted labels and attributed the "33" to the year that the Noble Experiment ended. Thus are legends born.

YUENGLING

By: D.G. Yuengling & Son
Where: Pottsville, PA
From: 1829–Present
Slogan: "America's Oldest Brewers"

Although the Yuengling brewery is only a two-and-a-half-hour drive from the heart of New York City, things in Pottsville are decidedly more rural than one would expect. My college friend, who does some business with the brewery, told me about a conversation he had with one of the executives of the company:

Friend: Say, I've got tickets to the Yankees—we should go sometime.
Yuengling: I don't particularly care for baseball.
Friend: How about football? I've got Giants seats also.
Yuengling: No, thanks. I don't care much for football, either.
Friend: Well, what kind of games *do* you like?
Yuengling: Boy, out here we like NASCAR—but it ain't no *game.*

NASCAR is certainly no game, and neither is Yuengling's emphasis on producing high-quality beer that everyone from racing fans to Wall Street executives can sink their teeth into. It was another German, David Yuengling, who started this quintessential American brewery, which was originally named the Eagle Brewery and whose trademark—a proud American eagle—still graces the Yuengling label today.

STRAUB

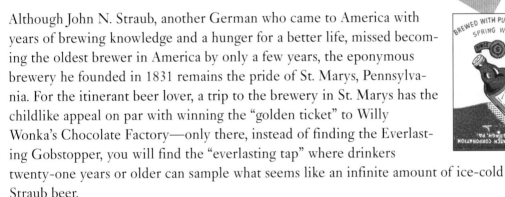

By: Straub Brewery
Where: St. Marys, PA
From: 1831–Present
Slogans: "Beer in All Its Glory!"
"The Natural Choice"

Although John N. Straub, another German who came to America with years of brewing knowledge and a hunger for a better life, missed becoming the oldest brewer in America by only a few years, the eponymous brewery he founded in 1831 remains the pride of St. Marys, Pennsylvania. For the itinerant beer lover, a trip to the brewery in St. Marys has the childlike appeal on par with winning the "golden ticket" to Willy Wonka's Chocolate Factory—only there, instead of finding the Everlasting Gobstopper, you will find the "everlasting tap" where drinkers twenty-one years or older can sample what seems like an infinite amount of ice-cold Straub beer.

Straub's secret to success lies in its natural brewing process, which uses no added sugar, salt, or preservatives—only fresh ingredients and spring water from the local Laurel Run Reservoir. As the country's smallest surviving pre-Prohibition brewery, Straub may be one of the last places where a beer lover can find a true, small regional brewery and experience a slice of American beer history firsthand. If you can't make it to the brewery, you can always grab a case of "greenies" (so named for their distinctive green bottles) on your way through the area and taste a beer that's "smooth, clean, and honestly fresh."

OLD MILWAUKEE

By: Jos. Schlitz Brewing Company (now Pabst Brewing Company)
Where: Milwaukee, WI
From: 1955–Present
Slogans: "It doesn't get any better than this!"
"America's Best Tasting Beer"

In 1955, Schlitz launched Old Milwaukee as "America's first popular beer." In other words, Old Milwaukee was created not to be an elite Bavarian-style pilsner, but to be a good, solid, inexpensive beer for the regular guy. And, after roughly fifty years, "OM" still is. Between its flagship Schlitz brand and the value-priced Old Milwaukee (among others), Schlitz Brewing stayed atop the brewing heap well into the 1960s.

If you're looking for proof of when America completely lost its sense of humor, look no further than the early 1990s and the introduction of the Old Milwaukee Swedish Bikini Team. Created by Hal Riney & Partners, the ad spots were highly sarcastic spoofs of the leading beer commercials of the day, in which a boring all-male vacation suddenly brightened with the unexplained appearance of scantily-clad, blond Swedish models with a cooler full of OM, ready to party.

After the Bikini Team's rapid rise in popularity, the female employees of then-owner Stroh Brewing filed a sexual harassment lawsuit, stating that the Team's "giggling, jiggling idiots with large breasts and small minds" helped create a hostile work atmosphere.

The company was eventually sold to the Stroh Brewing Company, which ended up in the hands of Pabst Brewing. Pabst's oddly successful formula for reinvigorating old brands has OM currently enjoying a resurgence—one that may possibly be led by the much maligned Swedish Bikini Team.

MILWAUKEE'S BEST

By: A. Gettelman Brewing Company (now Miller Brewing Company)
Where: Milwaukee, WI
From: 1895–Present

No doubt you have heard this fine brand referred to by its nickname (attributed, some say, to the aftereffects of consuming it): "Milwaukee's Beast" or, simply, "The Beast." Long appreciated by undergraduates for its drinkability and affordability, this value brand has been the star of many a college keg party and tailgate function. Back in the 1960s, the scare quotes around the word "best" on the label didn't help to reinforce the notion that Milwaukee's Best was indeed the town's leading beer.

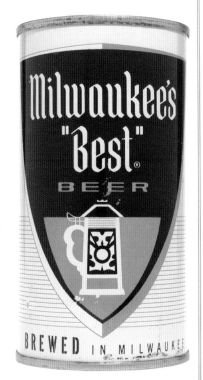

The A. Gettelman Brewery was established in 1887 and began producing "Gettelman's Milwaukee Best Beer" in 1895. It was only in 1956 that the "Milwaukee's Best" we know and love was introduced to America as a low-priced, full-flavor lager beer. The brand grew and, by 1961, had captured the eye of brewing behemoth Miller Brewing, who acquired the beer to complement its higher-priced Miller High Life brand. Unfortunately, the 1975 introduction of Miller Lite was so successful that Miller stopped production of Milwaukee's Best to focus on the massive Lite rollout. It was a long nine years for MB fans, but the brand made it back to store shelves in 1984.

OLD STYLE

By: G. Heileman Brewing Company
(now Pabst Brewing Company)
Where: La Crosse, WI
From: 1902–Present
Slogans: "Pure Brewed from God's Country"
"The Beer with the Old World Flavor"

Started as the City Brewery in 1858 by German immigrants Gottlieb Heileman and John Gund, the G. Heileman Brewing Company went on a 138-year run that only ended in 1996, when Stroh's purchased the company (later, Pabst Brewing acquired Stroh's). In 1983, the company—led by its premier brand, Old Style, which they began brewing in 1902—was the fourth largest brewer in the country and a billion dollar company. Although Heileman was proud brewer of the famous "big mouth" bottles of Mickey's Malt Liquor and Special Export, and eventual owner of Rainier, Heileman was most associated with Old Style Lager—Chicago's beer.

Whether you are on the north side or south side of Chicago, or "up north" in the Wisconsin woods, you are pretty much within spitting distance of an Old Style tap. A fixture at Cubs games since 1950, it is fair to say that every square inch of the legendary Wrigley Field has been baptized in the beer "brewed from God's Country." When sitting on the North Clark Street side of Wrigley and washing down a brat with an ice-cold Old Style, even die-hard New Yorkers like myself become Chicagoans for the day.

BERGHOFF

By: Huber Brewery
Where: Monroe, WI
From: 1887–Present
Slogan: "A Chicago Tradition Since 1887"

Brands like Berghoff prove that you didn't have to be from Milwaukee to make your fortune as a Bavarian brewer. Started in Wisconsin Territory in 1845 (three years before formal statehood in 1848), the Blumer Brewery in Monroe (now known as Huber Brewery) is the oldest continually operating brewery in the Midwest. Producing such classic brands as Berghoff Lager (1887) and Huber Premium Beer (1947), the Huber Brewery has been doing Wisconsin proud for over 160 years.

Although now well situated in metropolitan Chicago, Berghoff has never forgotten its rural roots. If you want proof of Berghoff's Wisconsin heritage, look no further than their annual sponsorship of the St. Germain Greater Wisconsin Muskie Tournament, which awards a thousand dollars plus a graphite replica of the prize catch to each year's winner.

LEINENKUGEL

By: Jacob Leinenkugel Brewing Company (now merged
    with Miller Brewing Company)
Where: Chippewa Falls, WI
From: 1867–Present
Slogan: "Chippewa Pride"

Slightly younger than its Wisconsin sister Huber, but with no less
    of a storied background, the Jacob Leinenkugel Brewing

Company of Chippewa Falls can be traced back to the early days
of Prussian settlement within the Wisconsin area. Starting out
in 1867 serving Leinenkugel beer to a thirsty, mostly all-male
population of nearly 3,000 lumberjacks, the Leinenkugel family's
brewery grew with the expansion of the North Woods around
them.

In the Native American Ojibwan tongue, "Wisconsin" means
"gathering of the waters." Appropriate, considering that it was the
waters of the Chippewa River that drew founder Jacob Leinenkugel
to set up shop back in 1867. These days, when you go "up north," do
not be surprised if you meet "Leine's" drinkers who would sooner go
blind than switch to Budweiser or other national brands. In fact, when doing research for
this book, I solicited opinions from over three hundred beer drinkers on their choice for
the Greatest American Beer. One Wisconsinite opined, "Friend, when the golden taste of
an ice cold Leine's first passes your lips, you will have no doubt as to what the winner will
be." After sampling a six-pack or two of this venerable brew, I find it hard to disagree!

POINT SPECIAL LAGER

By: Stevens Point Brewery
Where: Stevens Point, WI
From: 1857–Present
Slogans: "Brewing Excellence Since 1857"
"Point—Well Made."

1990 was a special year. The Hubble telescope was launched, Lech Walesa's Solidarity Party brought freedom to Poland, Nelson Mandela was finally released from prison—and Point beer was finally sold outside of Wisconsin for the first time. The collapse of the Soviet Union happened a year later, though it is still unclear what effect the Stevens Point Brewery had on the downfall of Communism. But for beer-loving Americans residing outside of the great state of Wisconsin, yet another classic beer became available.

Stevens Point, Wisconsin, has been known for its stellar Point Special Lager since 1857, making it the fifth oldest continuously operating brewery in the United States. Still a specialty beer with a relatively small production, Point Special is one of the oldest American beers to be brewed independently. At the time of this writing, the brewery is sponsoring a special concert featuring the unlikely combination of Rick Springfield, 38 Special, and Night Ranger—proving that this beer is still "motorin'."

NARRAGANSETT

By: Narragansett Brewing Company
Where: Cranston, RI
From: 1877–Present
Slogan: "Hi neighbor, have a 'Gansett."

Back in the 1950s, when Curt Gowdy was announcing Boston Red Sox games, almost every game was introduced with: "Hiya, neighbor. This is Red Sox baseball brought to you by Narragansett Lager Beer." At that time, Narragansett was New England's number one beer and outperformed Budweiser and Miller in certain areas of New England. At its height in the mid 1950s, the Narragansett Brewing Company occupied over a hundred acres of Cranston, Rhode Island.

Launched in Cranston in 1877 with seed money from top local businessmen, the company brought in a Berlin brewmaster, situated itself near a rail yard, and steadily reinvested its early profits in state-of-the-art bottling and refrigerated shipping systems. After steady growth through the early 1900s, the company managed to survive Prohibition by selling ice and "medicinal" products. In 1931, Narragansett joined forces with famed Boston brewer Rudolf F. Haffenreffer to further modernize the plant. By 1955, Narragansett was New England's number one beer.

In 1965, Falstaff Brewing bought the company, and Narragansett continued to have solid regional beer sales under Falstaff (and later, Pabst Brewing) but nothing like its Red Sox days. In 2003, after years of stagnant sales, the beer was sold to Miller Brewing Company. Today, thanks to local businessman—and current CEO—Mark Hellendrung, the Narragansett Brewing Company is back in local hands.

DIXIE

By: Dixie Brewing Company
Where: New Orleans, LA
From: 1907–Present
Slogan: "Happy Days with Dixie!"

Although selling cold beer in a tropical atmosphere seems like a
sure thing, New Orleans' Dixie Brewing is the last standing regional brewery of any signif-
icance in the state. Tracing its heritage back to 1907 when Valentine Merz opened the
brewing operation on Tulane Avenue, Dixie followed the pattern of many
regional brewers: solid growth up until Prohibition, hanging on through the dry
spell, reemerging after Prohibition, growth until the mid 1960s, and then
crushing defeat at the hands of the macrobrewers in the 1970s and beyond.
Dixie, however, managed to survive—and thrive—under the leadership of
owners Joe and Kendra Bruno, although it took a lot of work (and a bank-
ruptcy) to pull it off. The Dixie Brewing Company still brews its famous
Dixie Beer (now sold nationally), but it took the creation of "craft-
brewed" Blackened Voodoo Lager in 1990 to get the company back on
its feet. Much of the beer is still brewed in the gigantic cypress wood
tanks used over a hundred years ago, and hopefully the tradition will
continue long into the future. Since 2003, Dixie Brewing has been
part of Distinguished Brands International, the owner of specialty
brands including Czechvar, Erdinger, and Fuller's.

NATIONAL BOHEMIAN

By: National Brewing (now Pabst Brewing Company)
Where: Baltimore, MD
From: 1885–Present
Slogan: "From the Land of Pleasant Living"

The beer "from the land of pleasant living" is a Baltimore institution as strong as Old Bay Seasoning and the Orioles. Its history dates back to 1885 when the National Brewery launched the National Bohemian brand. The National Brewery itself was first erected in 1872 on Lager Beer Hill in Baltimore—so named for its beer storage ("lagering") cellars dug into the hillside as early as 1850. National Brewery really hit its stride right after Prohibition and continued strongly up until the 1960s, when over nine hundred people worked there to churn out such classic American brews as National Bohemian, National Premium, and even Colt 45 malt liquor. When National Brewing shut down in 1978, a proud Baltimore tradition of over 125 years died.

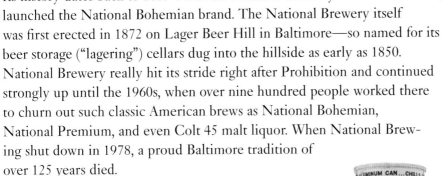

In 2001, the old Lager Beer Hill plant came back to life as a trendy office/condo complex—advertised with a National Bohemian banner strapped to the building's top floor. Now, "Natty Boh" is made under contract by Pabst Brewing at a Miller plant in North Carolina—far from Baltimore, but only a sip away from the land of pleasant living. . . .

MEISTER BRÄU

By: Peter Hand Brewing Company
     (then Miller Brewing Company)
Where: Chicago, IL
From: 1891–1989
Slogan: "The largest selling bottle beer in Chicago."

Translated from the German, *meister bräu* means "master's brew," but, in our ignorance, a friend and I always referred to it (with respect) as "Mister Beer." My introduction to this storied brand was in 1983, the year Miller Brewing re-introduced it into what parent company Philip Morris calls the "popular price" segment of the U.S. beer market. I had no idea back then what a rich history Meister Bräu had, and it was only later that I realized its major impact on the industry.

    In the brewing business, there is often a thin line between tremendous success and failure. For the Meister Bräu Brewing Company (formerly Peter Hand Brewing), the last surviving brewer in Chicago, inventing light beer in 1967 seemed like the start of something big. However, the company couldn't figure it out in time to avoid its demise. Basically, Meister Bräu bought the recipe for a "diet" beer called Gablinger's from Rheingold, and brought Meister Bräu Lite to the market, where it failed to catch on. When Miller Brewing bought the company five years later, in 1972, it renamed the light version of Meister Bräu "Lite Beer from Miller" and rolled out one of the most successful advertising campaigns in the history of man ("Great Taste … Less Filling"). Soon after, Lite was "everything you wanted in a beer … and less" and Meister Bräu was relegated to value-beer status until its eventual demise in 1989.

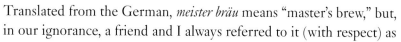

UTICA CLUB

By: Matt Brewing Company
Where: Utica, NY
From: 1888–Present
Slogans: "U.C. for me!"
"Tastiest Beer in Town"
"We still let nature make the beer, because that's the way you like it."

On April 7, 1933, Utica Club made history by being the first beer legally served after Prohibition ended. In fact, within one hour of its repeal, the Hotel Utica was serving Utica Club in its dining room. Seventy-three years later, the Matt Brewing Company is selling more upscale Saranac than Utica Club, but the legend lives on. As one of the few remaining privately held regional brewers, Matt Brewing still upholds the traditional craft brewing approach that began in the late nineteenth century with founder Francis Xavier "FX" Matt and is carried on today by his great-grandchildren.

Utica Club, which had stalled at around 400,000 barrels of beer a year, began an unlikely renaissance in 1959, spurred on by a set of talking beer mugs. The new UC spokesmugs, Schultz (an abrupt, Teutonic beer tankard sporting a Prussian war helmet) and Dooley (a stereotypical Irishman in the guise of an earthenware beer mug embellished with a shamrock) starred in a six-year advertising campaign that raised UC's production by nearly 200,000 barrels a year, a 50 percent increase. Voiced by Jonathan Winters, Schultz and Dooley were perhaps the earliest examples of comedic ads that beer companies turned to in order to boost sales (along with Piel's famous tandem of Bert and Harry). Today, original Schultz and Dooley mugs fetch upwards of a thousand dollars from breweriana collectors, and UC sales are up nine percent.

BILLY BEER

By: Falls City Brewing Company
Where: Louisville, KY
From: 1977–1978
Slogan: "Brewed expressly for and with the personal approval of one of America's all-time great beer drinkers—Billy Carter."

While Billy Beer was definitely *not* one of America's greatest beers, I've included it here because it was the thought that counted. For readers who don't recall, Billy Carter was the 1970s equivalent of Roger Clinton—kind of a redneck embarrassment that the president liked to break out in selected states during election years for populist appeal. Unfortunately for Jimmy Carter (who in 1977 was already saddled with the popular notion that he was the worst president ever), his Pabst-swigging brother, Billy, was talked into cashing in his folk hero appeal for the Falls City Brewing Company. The former gas station owner was suddenly the spokesmodel for Billy Beer, backed by advertising in which he proclaimed, "It's the best beer I've ever tasted—and I've tasted a lot." (It was a well known fact that Billy was actually a die-hard Pabst drinker and was rumored to have confided to friends that he didn't particularly care for his own brand.)

To many beer drinkers across America, this beer was the shining symbol of one of the biggest accomplishments a man could dream of: to drink so much beer that someone actually named one after you. Unfortunately for Billy, the beer itself didn't meet up with the marketing hype, and a series of bad publicity events doomed the beer to flash-in-the-pan status. The Falls City Brewing Company went with it, closing its doors in 1978.

SCHMIDT

By: Jacob Schmidt Brewing Company
(now Pabst Brewing Company)
Where: St. Paul, MN
From: 1844–Present
Slogans: "The Beer That Grew
with the Great Northwest"
"Official Beer of the American
Sportsman"

Just as the famous Rainier sign graced the skyline over Seattle for years, the famous "Schmidt" sign looked over the growing metropolis of St. Paul, Minnesota, for nearly fifty years, until 1990, when the historic Jacob Schmidt Brewery closed.

The "beer that grew with the great Northwest" was born in 1844, when the Northwest was sparsely populated, and did indeed grow along with a thirsty population of horsemen, fishermen, and hunters—a sporting image that Schmidt Beer embraced in its marketing during its heyday in the 1950s through the 1970s. Like many popular American brews, Schmidt changed hands a number of times through the course of its history: first, in 1955, when it was sold to the Pfeiffer Brewing Company, then in 1972 when it was bought by G. Heileman Brewing. A sad day for the beer came in 1993, when Heileman added an "s" to Schmidt Beer and started calling it "Schmidt's," the name of the historic Philadelphia brand it also brewed. The move saved the company's packaging costs, but at the expense of many Schmidt Beer purists. Eventually Stroh's acquired Heileman and, with it, the Schmidt brand. Now under Pabst ownership, the brand is attempting to reclaim its status as the "Official Beer of the American Sportsman" and the "s" has been removed from the label.

STAG

By: Neu and Gintz Brewery (now Pabst Brewing Company)
Where: Belleville, IL
From: 1851–Present
Slogans: "Stag Beer Makes Thirst a Pleasure"
　　　　　"The Monarch of Beers"

The largest selling brew in St. Louis in the 1940s and 1950s, Stag is remembered by its fans as the beer that "makes thirst a pleasure" and is one of the hallmark brands that was produced back when Belleville, Illinois, was one of the largest brewing centers in the country.

Founded in 1851 by Phillip Neu and Peter Gintz, the Neu and Gintz Brewery was largely unknown outside of Belleville and East St. Louis. After a string of successive owners, the brewery was renamed the Western Brewery in 1875 and eventually merged with the local Star Brewery in 1905. The beer that would become "Stag" was originally "Kaiser" beer. A spate of bad press for Germany's Kaiser Wilhelm slowed sales of the beer, and the brewer announced a naming contest in the local press. Belleville resident George Wuller took the twenty-five dollar prize for his suggestion of "Stag." The name stuck.

Stag's popularity attracted the interest of larger-than-life brewer Henry Louis Griesedieck, who purchased the brewery in 1912 and successfully grew the brand until Prohibition. Stag reemerged in 1933, under the helm of the newly formed Griesedieck–Western Brewing Company, and the brand continued to grow until Carling took over in 1954, heralding the beginning of Stag's greatest growth period. Stag eventually became popular enough to be operated as its own separate entity (Stag Brewing Company) from 1975 to 1979 and was later purchased by G. Heileman, which was bought by Stroh's and then by Pabst Brewing, where it remains today.

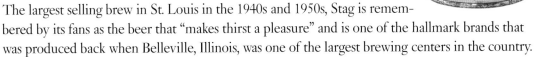

LUCKY LAGER

By: General Brewing Company
Where: San Francisco, CA
From: 1934–1978
Slogan: "The Age-Dated Beer"

The Lucky Lager story is refreshingly different from that of many of the great American beers featured in this book.

Started after Prohibition, the General Brewing Company was built from scratch by Adolphus Busch's grandson, Baron Paul C. Von Gontard (who was perhaps the first authentic modern-day Beer Baron). The factory was built specifically for Lucky Lager (with an anticipated first year capacity of 100,000 barrels), and the label was designed (by well-known advertising firm McCann Erickson) to stand out on the shelf and complement a large-scale advertising campaign. From the start, Lucky Lager was meant to be big and bold, just like the prominent red cross on its logo.

Following the Anheuser-Busch model, owner Gontard blitzed the market with lots of advertising, including magazine ads, billboards, and branded delivery trucks. Most of the ads featured a gimmick unheard of at the time: Lucky's version of "born-on" dating, in which every keg and can was prominently labeled to show the day it left the factory. The scheme seemed to work, and, by 1948, the brand was so big that General changed its name to Lucky Lager Brewing Company. Acquisitions in Los Angeles and Salt Lake City followed, and Lucky was soon the tenth largest brewer in the United States. In 1960, Lucky sponsored the Winter Olympics in Squaw Valley, California.

By 1970, Lucky's brand star faded considerably, and it was facing stiff competition from the major brewers. The brand limped along until 1978, when its lucky streak finally ended.

WEIDEMANN

By: George Weidemann Brewing Company
Where: Newport, KY
From: 1880–1983
Slogan: "Honest to Goodness Beer"

The Weidemann beer story is another tale of the intrepid German brewer seeking his fortune in America. This particular German, George Weidemann of Eisenach, made his way to New York in 1855 and quickly found employment in a Williamsburg brewery. Learning of a partnership opportunity below the Mason-Dixon line, Weidemann seized the opportunity and was soon installed as a co-partner in John Butcher's Newport, Kentucky, brewery, which was established in 1870. He bought the brewery outright in 1878 for the then-considerable sum of $28,000. Two years later, Weidemann bought another small Newport-based brewery and named his operation the George Weidemann Brewing Company.

By 1889, Weidemann had built the brewery into one of the most successful businesses in Northern Kentucky. When Weidemann died in 1890, he left his sons George and Charles a formidable business to run. Charles proved to be a heroic figure, risking his freedom to brew beer during Prohibition—an act that ultimately led to his arrest and would have led to his imprisonment had he not died before the start of his 1928 trial. That fate did not escape his son Carl, who was indicted on Prohibition charges and served two years in a federal penitentiary.

The Weidemann brewery eventually found its way into the hands of the G. Heileman Company, in 1967, where it was operated as the "Weidemann Division" and produced Weidemann Fine Beer and Blatz, among others. Heileman eventually decided to shutter the poorly performing Weidemann Division, and its signature beer with it, in 1983.

HOFBRAU

By: Horlacher Brewing Company
Where: Allentown, PA
From: 1897–1976
Slogan: "This is the original fine quality brew."

Born as the Allentown Brewing Company in 1897, the Horlacher Brewing Company (aka Hofbrau Brewing) was a prolific regional brewer with two primary brands in its portfolio: Horlacher, a fairly undistinguished lager, and Hofbrau, a similarly mediocre brew with a forty-year history. The company also had a couple short-lived experiences brewing both Holburg beer (1960–1970) and Rheinbeck Beer (1967–1970). However, the company experienced its main success selling private label brands for grocery stores.

Beginning in the 1930s, many "store brands" were produced for grocery stores, drug stores, convenience stores, and various bars and restaurants. Chains like 7-Eleven even had their own beer, as did supermarkets like Finast, Giant Foods, and Food Fair (Prize Beer). Back in the late 1960s, Horlacher produced Little King Beer for American Supermarkets, ShopRite Beer, and Pathmark Beer.

Brands like Pathmark and generic "Beer" came during the time when Americans first really started to question mass marketing and wonder just how much of a brand's marketing contributed to its price. "House" brands abounded like never before, offering the same great taste without the added marketing costs. In the case of Pathmark Beer, that taste was Hofbrau. Hey, if you were a regular Hofbrau drinker, you were making out like a bandit.

BARTELS

By: Bartels Brewing Company (now Lion Brewing Company)
Where: Syracuse, NY
From: 1893–present
Slogan: "There is none better."

Born in Richtenberg, Prussia, in 1853, Herman Bartels came to the United States in 1872 with plenty of brewing experience and quickly put it to use in the employ of several breweries, where he built a small nest egg. Initially investing it in Aurora, Illinois's Crescent Brewing Company, Bartels placed stakes on several Midwestern breweries and amassed enough to cash out and head to New York, where he was employed as the brewmaster for Syracuse's Haberle Brewing Company for six years. By the age of thirty-seven, Bartels had amassed enough wealth to purchase outright the neighboring John Greenway Brewery in 1893, and the Bartels Bewing Company was born. Not satisfied, Bartels also invested in a brewing operation in the Edwardsville section of Wilkes-Barre, Pennsylvania, and one in Rochester, New York (Monroe Brewing). Selling his namesake beer along with brands such as Crown and Old Devonshire, Bartels died in 1910 with a considerable upstate New York brewing empire, which passed along to his son.

Prohibition hit the second Bartels hard, however, causing his Monroe brewery to close. By 1942, the operation was already in decline, and that year saw the closing of the original Syracuse brewery. Yet, the Bartels brand still soldiered on.

Bartels's heyday came in the 1950s, when the Bartels "Professor," a somewhat stern, Germanic looking gentleman, was the brand's primary icon. The Edwardsville plant held on until 1968, when it was acquired by the Lion Brewing Company in Wilkes-Barre.

ORTLIEB'S

By: Henry F. Ortlieb Brewing Company
Where: Philadelphia, PA
From: 1866–1989
Slogans: "Philadelphia's Famous Beer"
"The Happiest Beer in Town!"

Philadelphians old enough to remember will forever mark 1981 as the year Ortlieb's closed its plant. Although Schmidt's, right up on Girard Street, still survived as Philly's last major brewer, the writing was on the wall for the city's once burgeoning brewing industry. Founded in 1869, the Ortlieb Brewery began its life at the birthplace of America lager: the very spot that John Wagner brewed America's first lager beer back in 1840.

Ortlieb's traces in origins back to 1866, when founder Trupert Ortlieb established a brewery on Third Street and Germantown Avenue in Philadelphia. In 1899, the brewery was named after his eldest son, Henry, who ran the business until he died in 1936. The brewery's presidency passed on to his brother, Joseph. Old "Uncle Joe" Ortlieb, who had worked at the plant since the tender age of fourteen, oversaw the period when Ortlieb's was big in Philadelphia. Under Uncle Joe's guidance, the beer went from 20,000 barrels a year before Prohibition to a height of over 500,000 barrels in 1954.

By the time Joseph Ortlieb took the helm in 1975, the major brewers had knocked Ortlieb's market share down significantly, changing it from a regional brewer into a truly local producer. Although Joe kept the plant busy contract-brewing beers like Olde English 800 and was quoted in the *Wall Street Journal* saying he would "rather fight [the major brewers] than fold," financial circumstances eventually forced a sale to Schmidt's in 1980. Schmidt's brewed Ortlieb's until 1987, and G. Heileman brewed it on a contract basis until 1989.

BUCKEYE

By: Buckeye Brewing Company
Where: Toledo, OH
From: 1838–1971
Slogan: "It's Kraeusened"

Although Ohio never gained the beer-making prominence of other Midwestern states such as Wisconsin and Missouri, it was able to boast of its famous Buckeye beer. And when the most famous celebrity from Toledo, Ohio, is Jamie Farr (of M*A*S*H fame), having your own beer is something to shout about. Launched in 1838 on the corner of Front and Consul Street in downtown Toledo, the Buckeye Brewing Company eventually moved to the intersection of Bush and Champlain, where it remained for 134 years. Although some later advertising attributes the date 1872 as the genesis of the Buckeye operation (when new owners Jacobi and Coughlin bought the brewery from its previous owners), Buckeye can accurately claim 1838 as its true birth year—making it one of the oldest American beers.

Since its inception, Buckeye used kraeusening in the brewing process: a portion of partially fermented wort (the sugary beer extract) was added to produce a secondary fermentation. This traditional Bavarian brewing method gave Buckeye a distinctive flavor—and a unique marketing angle. Few Toledo residents were able to accurately define "kraeusening" but, by God, it made for a tasty beer! Unfortunately for Buckeye, the angle was not enough to sustain Toledo's brewing industry. By 1949, Buckeye was the last brewery standing in the city, and, by 1971, the old Buckeye plant was torn down.

OLDE FROTHINGSLOSH

By: Pittsburgh Brewing Company
Where: Pittsburgh, PA
From: 1950–Present
Slogan: "Whale of an Ale for the Pale Stale Male"

I have included Olde Frothingslosh in *Great American Beer* partly because of popular demand—but mostly because the very idea of the brand embodies the essence of what makes American beer so great in the first place. Olde Frothingslosh was the genesis of all the novelty beers to follow—from Billy Beer to generic "Beer" and everything in between.

Olde Frothingslosh was created in the early 1950s by morning radio man Rege Cordic, who created a variety of put-on commercials to amuse his Pittsburgh-based KDKA radio audience. Among them was one for Olde Frothingslosh, the "Whale of an Ale for the Pale Stale Male." Cordic and his on-air comedy team obliged listeners with fables regarding the beer's incredible history and unique properties. It was a beer so light that refrigerator cars weighed less filled with Olde Frothingslosh than when empty—and the only beer with the foam on the *bottom* of the glass. The absurd take-up rose to new heights as the comedy team recorded commercials for the beer and staged a series of historical photos depicting the difficulty of producing a beer that light.

What made the whole gag truly fun was when Pittsburgh Brewing President, S. E. Cowelt, a regular listener to the show, actually decided to make it by putting Iron City into special cans. Ever since then, a special edition of Olde Frothingslosh comes out during the Christmas holiday—and sells like wildfire in Pittsburgh. Old cans of this limited edition beer are prized collector's items.

Resources and Ephemera

BeerBooks.com
BeerBooks.com's mission is to bring beer enthusiasts together with the books they love, and this informative site does all that—and more. The website not only puts all the beer titles you'll ever want to read in one place but also features links and information on all of the beer-related resources you would ever need.

All About Beer magazine
www.allaboutbeer.com
For twenty-two years running, *All About Beer* magazine has ruled as the definitive source for beer information. Each issue is packed with entertaining features, the best beer reviews, and the most cutting-edge beer news. Visit their website for information on beer travel and events, merchandise, homebrewing, and more.

TavernTrove.com
Did you know that every single image in this book is available for purchase through Tavern Trove, one of the most comprehensive websites dedicated to selling breweriana items? Owner Erik Amundson scours the country in search of breweriana and has amassed a pretty large collection of rare beer cans and bottles, beer trays, matchbooks, great old print ads, beer signs, can openers, and just about anything you can think of that has a beer brand associated with it. Whether you are interested in buying or just searching the site for fun, Tavern Trove is a good stop on the Web.

Beer Cap Puzzle (Rebus) Solutions
www.geocities.com/shabber_1/rainier.html
Solutions to puzzles on Rainier, Pearl, Olympia, and Lucky Lager bottle caps.

Ballantine-Specific Puzzle Solutions
www.mistrettas.com/body_rebus.html

Beer Can Trash
www.rustycans.com/tossed.html
Interesting observations on how canning changed the beer industry—and the merits of canned beer, explained by a 1940s era Blatz can.

BeerHistory.com
Some people are more interested in drinking beer than learning about it. But for those who find themselves bitten by the history bug, there is BeerHistory.com, a site dedicated to—yes, you guessed it—the history of beer. Great articles by beer historian Carl H. Miller, lots of incredible reference material, and a superb collection of beer books available for sale.

Black Label History and Fan Site
members.tripod.com/corzman69/id23.htm
The history of the brand, along with some great vintage photos, by Charlie Smigo, aka "Corzman69," probably the greatest fan of the brand (and an apt historian as well). Be sure to check out his personal page ("About Corzman69").

H.O. Scale Beer-Themed Model Railroad Cars
www.hobeercars.com
An extremely vertical site, dedicated to collectors of H.O. scale model railroad cars. An unbelievable collection of brands are available, and the site is worth viewing, whether or not you have the slightest interest in collecting model trains.

RustyCans.com
Everything you wanted to know about beer can collecting, from an avid collector and amateur beer historian. Fabulous collection of store brands.

Bibliography and Selected Reading

BOOKS

Apps, Jerry. *Breweries of Wisconsin, Second Edition.* University of Wisconsin Press, 2005.

Baron, Stanley Wade. *Brewed in America: The History of Beer and Ale in the United States.* Little Brown & Co., 1962.

Blum, Peter H. *Brewed in Detroit: Breweries and Beers Since 1830.* Wayne State University Press, 1999.

Cochran, Thomas C. *The Pabst Brewing Company: History of an American Business.* New York University Press, 1948.

Cushman, Gary and Russ Hammer, et al. *New England Breweriana.* Schiffer Publishing, 2001.

Eames, Alan D. *Secret Life of Beer: Legends, Lore & Little-Known Facts.* Storey Books, 1995.

Flanagan, John T. *Theodore Hamm in Minnesota: His Family and Brewery.* Pogo Press, 1989.

The F. & M. Schaefer Brewing Company: To Commemorate Our 100th Year. F. & M. Schaefer Brewing Company, 1942.

Griesedieck, Alvin. *The Falstaff Story.* Simmons-Sissler Co., 1953.

Guetig, Peter R. and Conrad D Selle. *Louisville Breweries: A History of the Brewing Industry in Louisville, Kentucky.* Mark Skaggs Press, 1995.

Harris, Moira F. *The Paws of Refreshment: The Story of Hamm's Beer Advertising.* Pogo Press, 2000.

John, Tim. *The Miller Beer Barons: The Frederick J. Miller Family and Its Brewery.* Badger Books, 2005.

Koeller, Paul D. and David H. Delano. *Brewed with Style: The Story of the House of Heileman.* University of Wisconsin–La Crosse Foundation, 2004.

Meier, Gary and Gloria. *Brewed in the Pacific Northwest: A History of Beer Making in Oregon and Washington.* Fjord Press, 1991.

Musson, M.D., Robert A. *Brewing Beer in the Buckeye State, Volume 1: A History of the Brewing Industry in Eastern Ohio from 1808 to 2004.* Zepp Publications, 2005.

Noon, Mark A. *Yuengling: A History of America's Oldest Brewery.* McFarland & Company, Inc., 2005.

Plavchan, Ronald Jan. *A History of Anheuser-Busch, 1852–1933.* Arno Press, 1969.

Skilnik, Bob. *History of Beer and Brewing in Chicago: Volume II.* Infinity Publishing, 2002.

Smith, Gregg. *Beer in America: The Early Years, 1587–1840.* Brewers Publications, 1998.

Van Wieren, Dale P. *American Breweries II.* Eastern Coast Breweriana Association, 1995.

Walker, Stephen P. *Lemp: The Haunting History, Revised Edition.* Lemp Preservation Society, 2004.

ARTICLES

Hofmann, Rolf. "From Ludwigsburg to Brooklyn—A Dynasty of German–Jewish Brewers." *Aufbau,* 2001.

Holland, Gerald. "The King of Beer." *The American Mercury,* 1929.

Miller, Carl H. "Adolphus Busch: Captain of Industry." *BeerHistory.com,* 2005.

Miller, Carl H. "Beer and Television: Perfectly Tuned In." *All About Beer Magazine,* 2002.

Miller, Carl H. "Labor in the Brewery." *BeerHistory.com,* 2005.

Miller, Carl H. "The Rise of the Beer Barons." *All About Beer Magazine,* 1999.

Modern Brewery Age. "Top 10 U.S. Brewers in 1997." *Modern Brewery Age,* 1997 Statistical Review Edition.

*When life at its best
calls for beer at its best…
This is the one for you!*

FALSTAFF! Clear, golden, mellow as firelight.

List of Illustrations

Page 55: *Left:* This porcelain Hamm's Bear stands six inches tall and was made by the Hamm's Collectors Club in 1999. *Right:* Hamm's was one of the largest brewers in the United States when this 12-ounce bottle was produced in 1961.

Page 56: A late 1940s coaster introducing Michelob as the premium brand of the Anheuser-Busch Brewing Company.

Page 57: This 12-ounce Michelob "Contoured Can" was used for only a short time in the early 1970s.

Page 58: Detail of a Ballantine magazine advertisement from the late 1940s.

Page 59: A 1958 Ballantine coaster.

Page 60: *Left:* An Iron City Lager 4-inch coaster from 1945. *Right:* A 1962 12-ounce Iron City "Snap Top" can.

Page 61: A 1975 Iron City can featuring the Pittsburgh Steelers on a special run of Super Bowl cans.

Page 62: A 12-ounce Schaefer beer can used from 1968–1971.

Page 63: A 12-ounce Schaefer beer can used in the early 1940s.

Page 64: A 1978 Rheingold coaster.

Page 65: *Left:* A 12-ounce Rheingold can used by the United States Brewing Company of Chicago in the early 1950s. *Right:* An early 1960s-era 12-ounce can from the New Jersey branch of the New York–based Rheingold brewery.

Page 66: *Left:* A 1950s Blatz coaster. *Right:* This 12-ounce Blatz can dates from 1936 and is valued at about $350.

Page 67: A Blatz beer advertisement from the autumn of 1947.

Page 68: This Falstaff quart bottle is from around 1948.

Page 69: Detail of a Falstaff magazine advertisement from 1956.

Page 70: *Left:* A 3½-inch Piels coaster from 1957 featuring Bert and Harry Piel. One of a six coaster set. *Center:* An early 1960s Piels beer tray. *Right:* A 12-ounce Piels beer can from 1963.

Page 71: Bert and Harry Piel in a 13-inch Piel's tray from 1957.

Page 72: A 12-ounce Carling Black Label can from 1968.

Page 73: A 1970s-era Carling Black Label can.

Page 74: *Left:* A Coors bottle cap (or "crown") from the 1940s. *Right:* Coors pioneered aluminum beverage containers with this 7-ounce can from 1959.

Page 75: A 1936–38 Coors coaster.

Page 78: A Löwenbräu beer can from Germany, circa 1967.

Page 79: *Top and bottom:* The front and back view of a Ruppert Knickerbocker coaster from about 1968.

Page 80: A 12-ounce Grain Belt can from 1964.

Page 81: *Left:* A Stroh's beer tray from 1979. *Center:* A Stroh's bottle cap from the late 1940s. *Right:* A 12-ounce Stroh's beer can from 1956.

Page 82: This can-shaped Olympia Beer decal was produced in 1976.

Page 83: *Left:* Detail of a 1930s-era Rainier Beer matchbook. *Above right:* A 12-ounce Rainier Light beer can from 1967. *Below Right:* An unused Rainier bottle cap from the 1930s.

Page 84: *Left:* A Genessee 12-inch beer tray from 1953. *Right:* A 12-ounce Genesee Ale can from 1960.

Page 85: A 1953 Genesee beer tray liner (inside a vintage Genesee tray).

Page 86: A Lone Star beer patch from around 1970.

Early American News

This is the *light ale* millions of present-day Americans prefer to beer

THE *lightness* of Ballantine's Ale comes as a pleasant surprise to those who still think that ale's on the "heavy" side.

But it's the Ballantine *flavor* that has won beer drinkers so completely . . . a flavor so superb that it could come only from the very finest of *ale* yeasts.

Join the Ballantine regulars in a glass today—and chances are you'll decide that from now on you're an ale man yourself.

Look for the famous 3-RING trademark standing for PURITY, BODY, FLAVOR; and call for Ballantine's Ale. Costs no more than the better beers. Sold coast to coast.

BALLANTINE'S ALE

America's largest selling Ale

About the Authors

CHRISTOPHER B. O'HARA is the author of books *The Bloody Mary*, *Ribs*, *The Ultimate Chili Book*, *Hot Toddies*, and *Wing It!* Chris and his books have been featured on the Food Network's *Cooking Today* and *Sara's Secrets*, NBC's *Today Show*, CBS's *Early Show*, and periodicals including the *New York Post*, the *Boston Herald*, the *Miami Herald*, *Glamour*, and *Playboy* magazine. He lives in Lloyd Harbor, New York, with his wife, Jennifer, and children, C.J. and Holland. This is his third book for Clarkson Potter. He can be contacted through his website, www.chrisohara.com.

ALETHEA WOJCIK pursues photography as a passion and a profession. A native of New York state and a graduate of the Massachusetts College of Art, Ms. Wojcik moved to New York City in 1997, where she has since created a diverse and striking portfolio. She is active in both digital and traditional media, and her photographs can be seen in a variety of regional and national publications. A portrait artist and still-life specialist, Alethea Wojcik's work has appeared in New York and Boston exhibitions.

Grateful acknowledgment is made to Dale P. Van Wieren
for permission to reprint the following material in edited
form: Chronology of the American Brewing Industry from
the book *American Breweries II.*

PUBLISHED IN THE UNITED STATES BY

Clarkson Potter/Publishers,
an imprint of the Crown Publishing Group,
a division of Random House, Inc., New York.
www.crownpublishing.com
www.clarksonpotter.com

Clarkson N. Potter is a trademark and Potter
and colophon are registered trademarks of
Random House, Inc.

DESIGN BY Jennifer K. Beal

Library of Congress Cataloging-in-Publication Data
O'Hara, Christopher B.
Great American beer: 50 brands that shaped the
20th century/Christopher B. O'Hara; photographs by
Alethea Wojcik.—1st ed.
Includes bibliographical references.
1. Beer industry—United States—History.
2. Beer—United States.   I. Title.
HD9397.U52O38   2006
338.7'663420973—dc22
2005025038

ISBN-13: 978-0-307-23853-5
ISBN-10: 0-307-23853-9

Printed in Singapore

10 9 8 7 6 5 4 3 2 1

First Edition